Useless, but interesting Facts

By

René Lauritsen

Useless, but interesting Facts

A Collection of Curious Curiosities

Made by
René Lauritsen

...It's not that useless, is it??

We all have a lot of knowledge stored in the back of our minds that we've accumulated over time. Most of it is not something we actively use in our daily lives, but it still forms an understanding of the world we live in and the people around us. This book takes it a step further with interesting facts that you surely didn't know about. You will be both entertained and amazed as you read this book.

Reality usually surpasses imagination

The world is filled with stories and facts that are incredible, fantastic, and shocking. This book is packed with such content and is guaranteed to fascinate you. I've fact-checked as thoroughly as possible, and even though many pieces of information seem far-fetched, they are nonetheless true.

Some facts are short, others are longer, and there's something for everyone, providing exciting conversation topics for any occasion and food for thought.

... so lean back, relax, and enjoy the book.

Best Regards,

René Lauritsen

I am sure you will find this book interesting and informative.

If so, please consider giving it a review on Amazon and perhaps mention it or link to it on your social medias.

Thanks, it will be highly appreciated.

1. In 1996, the Canadian Brian Zembic made a bet. He was to get breast implants and wear them for at least one year to win.

Brian, who loves betting and gambling, went to a surgeon and asked if he would implant them on him. The surgeon asked if it was a bet. In fact, the surgeon and Brian played backgammon to decide the payment for the breasts. Brian won.

Brian was supposed to have the implants for 1 year, but because of all the attention he received, he kept them for 20 years and only had them removed in 2016.

2. 'Phantom vibration syndrome' or 'Fantom vibrations syndrom' is the perception that your mobile phone is ringing or vibrating when it is not, in reality, doing so. It's a kind of hallucination. Up to 90 percent of people have experienced thinking their phone is ringing or vibrating, especially when it's in their pocket. This phenomenon occurs after having a phone for anywhere between 1 month to 1 year. You're not going crazy; it's perfectly normal.

3. The title for the worst parents of the decade goes to a South Korean couple. They starved their three-month-old child to death. This is because they spent all their time in internet cafes playing a game called Prius Online.

The game involved taking care of a virtual child

4. A woman in the USA did not want to continue living in the city where she and her husband resided, but the husband did not want to move. One day, she called the police and reported a break-in, with an assault and rape on her.

It turned out not to be true; it was fabricated to persuade her husband to move. She even had a friend hit her, make a cut with a knife, and even wet her pants, all to make it look genuine.

The couple is now divorced.

5. North Korea briefly establish its own time zone (known as Pyongyang Time) in 2015 which was 30 minutes behind South Korea, they reverted back to Korea Standard Time (matching South Korea's time zone) in 2018.

6. One doesn't need to eat fruits and vegetables; one can actually live without them.

Inuits in Greenland did not have access to fruits and vegetables and managed to survive. Instead, they consumed the animals' innards. For instance, there are plenty of vitamins in the intestines, liver, kidneys, and heart, while testicles contain zinc and magnesium

7. The word "inuit" denotes the indigenous people of the Arctic region. The word means "the people." A single person is called "inuk."

The Inuit did not live in igloos. They lived in tents made of skins or houses of turf. Igloos were used for a few days when hunters were on trips or hunting. Igloos were practical as they could be built quickly, they provided shelter from wind and snow - and yes, they probably kept the beers nice and cold.

8. North Korea has claimed the wildest things. Their now-deceased leader Kim Jong Il claimed to have written 1,500 books in three years, invented the hamburger, and hit 11 hole-in-ones in a row in golf — notably, the first time he ever played golf.

North Korean scientists claimed in 2012 that unicorns exist in North Korea.

9. On average, the human body contains about 8.8 ounces (or approximately half a pound) of salt. This is equivalent to around 3.5 ounces of sodium. However, this amount can differ depending on a person's size and diet.

Sodium plays a pivotal role in our body's physiology. It's crucial for transmitting nerve signals, ensuring we maintain the right fluid balance, and enabling muscle contractions.

When we look at where sodium is located in the body, most of it resides in our blood and the fluids surrounding our cells.

10. It takes approximately eight hours for a brass door handle to disinfect itself. This is due to the toxic effect the metal has on viruses and bacteria (Including COVID)

11. The Tour de France was established in 1903, actually as a publicity stunt for a newspaper. Almost half of the participants in the first race were disqualified. Not for using doping, but for having traveled part of the route by car or train.

12. The oldest hotel in the world is "Nishiyama Onsen Keiunkan". It opened in the year 705 AD and has since been operated by 52 generations of the same family. Now that's what you can call a family business.

13. Harry Houdini claimed that he could withstand any punch to the stomach and even used this claim in his performances. Shortly before his death, J. Gordon Whitehead delivered several blows to his abdomen. However, Houdini experienced intense pain and stopped Gordon from striking further.

He continued to experience significant pain, and when he finally sought medical attention a few days later, the doctor diagnosed Houdini with appendicitis. He died a few days later, on October 31, 1926, at Detroit's

Grace Hospital. He was 52 years old. It remains uncertain whether the punches caused his death or if he would have died anyway since he refused to undergo an appendectomy.

14. The first person to "sail" down Niagara Falls in a barrel was Annie Edson Taylor. She was facing financial difficulties and expected to make good money from this stunt.

She survived and said she'd rather be blown up than do it again. She became well-known, but didn't make much money from it. Her manager ran off with the barrel Annie had used, and she spent most of the money she earned on detectives to find it.

15. Bobby Leach was the first man to go down Niagara Falls in a barrel. This happened on July 25, 1911. After this stunt, he had to stay in the hospital for 6 months due to the injuries he sustained. Both of his knees were broken, as was his jaw. For years, he traveled around Canada, England, and the USA to showcase the barrel, talk about the event, and sell pictures.

He died on April 26, 1926. This occurred during a trip to New Zealand, where he slipped on an orange peel and injured one of his legs.

Despite medical attention, gangrene set into the leg which subsequently had to be amputated. Nevertheless, he died shortly afterward due to complications.

16. It's a myth that dogs are colorblind and only see black/gray, but they do see colors worse than humans.

17. As we know, smell arises when molecules float in the air and into our nose.

But just consider that from there, they are sucked further down into our lungs where the molecules can enter the bloodstream. Now think about the fact that researchers believe we inhale up to a liter of intestinal gases a day. Bon appétit!

18. It's cheaper to buy a Greek island than to purchase an apartment in central London.

19. In connection with the first manned spaceflights, astronauts couldn't obtain life insurance that would support their families if they were killed.

Some of the astronauts came up with the idea to sign their autographs on numerous postcards. The idea was that these could become very valuable if the astronauts died.

20. Mao Zedong, China's communist leader, never took a bath or brushed his teeth. Poor young girls he surrounded himself with, who were expected to be available for his sexual desires.

Mao despised sparrows because they consumed grain, which he didn't want. He intended to export the grain to get money to develop the country.

He launched a campaign against sparrows and everyone was encouraged to kill as many as possible.

This resulted in an explosion of insect populations, which damaged the crops even more than the sparrows would have.

Up to 40 million Chinese died from hunger. After this, it is said that Mao wrote a letter to Stalin asking him to send 200,000 sparrows. He did not comply to the request.

21. Andy Warhol's real name was Andrew Warhola. Perhaps that's not as surprising as Kirk Douglas' real name: Issur Danielovitch. Try pronouncing that!

22. If you have a dog, and especially if you're elderly or ill, I think you should be aware of the following unsettling, yet intriguing fact.

Carolyn Rando is a forensic scientist and has seen quite a lot. She says that your dog might very well eat you if you were to die, and a lot quicker than you might think. They usually start with the cheeks, eyes, and then move on to the rest of the face.

She recounted a case where a woman had been dead for about a month before being found. Her two dogs had feasted on her. Someone with a morbid sense of humor might call them well-mannered dogs, as they had nearly finished everything - only hair, skull, and a few bones remained.

23. James Gorden once owned a 100-meter long yacht. Inside the yacht, there was a stable for a single cow. The reason was so that James could have fresh milk.

24. In 1958, Chinese leader Mao Zedong met with the Soviet Union's leader, Nikita Khrushchev. Both countries were communist, but the friendship between them had faded. Nikita aimed to move towards friendlier relations with non-communist nations, while Mao had a much more aggressive approach to the matter.

The parties maintained a facade and met on various occasions. During a meeting hosted by Mao in August 1958, Mao decided to lighten the mood. They were to take a swim in Mao's swimming pool.

This might sound pleasant enough, except for the fact that Nikita couldn't swim at all, and Mao was fully aware of this. It resulted in an awkward situation where Mao energetically swam back and forth while Nikita floundered around.

25. One would think Putin had read about the previous episode because he did something undeniably reminiscent of it.

In 2006, Putin had Germany's Angela Merkel on a state visit in Moscow. During the meeting, Putin's dogs were also present. Merkel certainly doesn't like dogs and hasn't since she was bitten by one as a child.

26. A typical house cat usually sleeps 16 hours a day. That's close to the world's laziest animal. Sloths sleep between 16-20 hours a day.

27. The first woman to cross the channel between England and France was the 20-year-old swimmer Gertrude Ederle. She accomplished this feat in August 1926.

28. There were many versions of "Little Red Riding Hood" before the Grimm brothers modified the tale to the one we recognize today. And fortunately so, otherwise many educators might choke on their coffee while reading the story aloud.

In a French version, the wolf tricked Little Red Riding Hood into eating her grandmother's flesh and drinking her blood.

The wolf then convinced Little Red Riding Hood to undress and get into bed with him (at this point, some might find the story intriguing, but they should certainly be ashamed of themselves). However, she went outside to urinate. Impatient, the wolf called out to her, but Little Red Riding Hood had run away - without even saying goodbye.

29. A Kibbutz is a type of collective in Israel, established in 1909. It began as an agricultural venture, but has since evolved to include factories as well.

One successful invention that originated from a Kibbutz is the "epilator", an electronic device that women use for hair removal. The first version was made in Israel in 1986.

30. Air travel is popular. On average, there are always around 500,000 people in the air worldwide.

31. There are six Nobel Prize categories:

- Nobel Prize in Physics
- Nobel Prize in Chemistry
- Nobel Prize in Physiology or Medicine
- Nobel Prize in Literature
- Nobel Peace Prize
- Nobel Prize in Economics

Alfred Nobel invented dynamite and established the Nobel Prizes to create a more positive legacy for himself.

32. The city of Edinburgh in Scotland is built on an inactive volcano.

33. The utterly insane dictator Josef Stalin wanted to create a new type of soldiers in the 1920s—a cross between humans and apes. He ordered scientist Ilya Ivanov to produce this new kind of soldier. These soldiers were supposed to be extraordinarily aggressive, better at enduring pain, and capable of eating almost anything.

Both Ivanov and Stalin were atheists, and based on the theory of evolution, humans and apes were believed to be related. It was a prevailing notion back then that Africans were more closely related to apes than the rest of humanity.

Ivanov was sent to Africa to conduct experiments involving inseminating chimpanzees with human sperm. A facility was established in Georgia. The offspring was meant to grow up and be trained as super soldiers.

However, this endeavor turned out to be a failure, as nothing came out of these deranged experiments. Later, there was an attempt to experiment with inseminating volunteer women with ape sperm. This too failed. Ivanov was imprisoned for his futile efforts.

34. The American magazine "Time Magazine" had Adolf Hitler on the cover as the "Man of the Year" in 1938 and wrote an article about him.

However, it should be noted that they did not endorse his views and in the article referred to him as the greatest threat to the democratic world.

35. The world's largest cattle station is located in Australia and is larger than the nation of Israel.

36. Three of Fidel Castro's sons, Alexis, Alexander, and Alejandro, are named after Alexander the Great.

37. Historians and scholars of religion agree that Jesus was not born on December 24th or in December at all. Nobody knows when he was actually born, as birthdays were not celebrated back then and the date was not considered important.

The decision to celebrate Jesus' birth on December 25th was made in the 4th century. In Denmark, his birthday is celebrated on December 24th because the day didn't start at midnight as it does today; it started at sunset.

Furthermore, Jesus was not born in the year 0. In fact, there is no such thing as the year 0. There is 1 BC (Before Christ) and 1 AD (Anno Domini, meaning "In the year of our Lord"). But there is no year 0.

38. The man who designed Saddam Hussein's bunker in Baghdad was the grandson of the woman who designed Hitler's bunker in Berlin.

39. Leonardo Da Vinci (April 15, 1452, to May 2, 1519) was left-handed and a vegetarian. He was the first Italian to use oil painting. He detested war but invented weapons.

Leonardo was dyslexic, which made reading his notes difficult. He exhumed bodies from graveyards to study human anatomy.

40. During your lifetime, you have produced enough saliva to fill two swimming pools.

41. In the field of statistics, the goal is to identify relationships among various factors (variables). Statistics are used to arrive at explanations and, consequently, solutions.

I've looked at the global situation and believe I have the solution to bring peace to the world.

If we examine the world and identify regions with conflicts and wars, a correlation becomes apparent.

In the majority of these troubled countries, the consumption of bacon, sausages, and alcohol is restricted.

From a statistical perspective, one could conclude that IF we could all enjoy some good bacon, grill some sausages, and share some beer, we might achieve world peace. Just regular Danish coziness for everyone.

PS: Hitler was a vegetarian and abstained from alcohol. That's something to ponder.

42. Bikinis and tampons were invented by men. The bikini is named after the Bikini Atoll, where atomic bomb tests were conducted. The idea was that the bikini would have the same "explosive" effect on men as an atomic bomb.

The term "tampon" can be traced back to medieval French and translates to "a plug of material for stopping a hole."

Something explosive and something for plugging dirty holes – indeed, quite fitting names.

43. Messages from the brain travel at speeds of over 300 km/h through the nervous system.

44. There are more sheep and lambs in New Zealand than humans

45. If you run in the rain, you will get wetter than if you walk. When you run in the rain, you expose yourself to a greater amount of raindrops hitting your body in a shorter period of time compared to walking. This increases the impact and force of the raindrops, causing more water to make contact with your body and clothing.

46. Getting married usually only requires a signature from both parties in most places.

However, the situation is different in the Indian state of Madhya Pradesh. The groom must prove that his home is equipped with a toilet. Yes, a toilet, but why?

Lack of toilets is a problem in India. According to the World Toilet Organization (yes, such an organization exists), there are over 2 billion people worldwide without access to toilets. This contributes to a significant number of deaths, especially among children.

If you absolutely MUST know, the website for the World Toilet Organization is: www.WorldToilet.org

47. In Japan, you can buy melons that are shaped like pyramids.

48. In the Czech Republic, there is a Roman Catholic chapel called Sedlec Ossuary. It contains tens of thousands of bones that are used for decoration. Among other things, the chandelier in the chapel is made from human bones.

The Sedlec Ossuary, also known as the "Church of Bones," is located in Kutná Hora, Czech Republic. It is a unique and somewhat macabre example of religious artwork. The ossuary contains the remains of an estimated 40,000 to 70,000 individuals, and the bones have been artistically arranged to create various decorations and structures, including a chandelier made from human bones. The ossuary is a popular tourist attraction and is known for its eerie yet fascinating atmosphere.

49. In New York, it is illegal to sell a house that is haunted by ghosts without first informing the buyer about it.

While the legality of disclosing paranormal activity when selling a house can vary by jurisdiction, some places do indeed have laws or regulations that require sellers to disclose certain types of information to potential buyers, including if a property is believed to be haunted. This is done to ensure transparency and to allow buyers to make informed decisions about their purchase. Whether or not one believes in ghosts, disclosing such information can be seen as a way to provide full information about the property's history and any potential concerns.

50. Are you going on vacation in New York and trying all the restaurants there? The city has so many restaurants that if you eat at a restaurant every night, it would take you over 50 years to try them all.

51. Approximately 40% of Australia is dominated by arid deserts, presenting a starkly different environment from what you might be accustomed to. These deserts showcase the raw beauty of nature, with their sweeping dunes, expansive plains, and unique plant and animal life that have evolved to adapt to the harsh conditions.

What's even more intriguing is the fact that Australia boasts not just one or two, but a total of three distinct deserts. Each desert is a testament to the country's vast and varied geographical tapestry. These deserts—like the Simpson Desert, the Great Victoria Desert, and the Tanami Desert—carry their own stories etched in the shifting sands and rugged terrains.

52. The highest temperature ever recorded was in the Lut Desert in Iran. A NASA satellite measured a temperature of 70.7 degrees Celsius (159.3 degrees Fahrenheit) in 2005. Sunscreen with a minimum SPF of 2000 would be a wise choice.

53. The wristwatch was invented in Switzerland. It was Abraham-Louis Breguet who created the first one in 1810. However, it took a long time for wristwatches to become popular among men, as they were initially perceived as feminine due to their association with bracelets.

It wasn't until after World War I that a shift occurred. Soldiers had used wristwatches, but it was when it became known that pilots used them that men started embracing the idea. Wearing a pocket watch was impractical for pilots, and since pilots were highly admired, the trend caught on. If pilots could benefit from wristwatches, men were eager to adopt the concept as well.

54. Some sharks have to keep swimming constantly. Day and night, without stopping. This is because these types of sharks need to have water constantly flowing over their gills to extract oxygen from the water.

55. The first railroad networks in the United States were primarily built by Chinese immigrants.

The construction of the Transcontinental Railroad in the 19th century involved a significant workforce of Chinese immigrants who played a crucial role in building the railroad tracks, particularly the western portion. The Central Pacific Railroad, which was responsible for laying tracks from the west coast towards the east, relied heavily on Chinese laborers to perform the demanding and often dangerous work of blasting tunnels through mountains, grading the land, and laying tracks. Their contributions were essential in connecting the eastern and western parts of the United States by rail

56. In the year 1800, there were approximately 1 billion people in the world. From the year 1900, when the population reached 1.5 billion, the growth rate accelerated significantly despite various global wars.

By 1950, the world population had risen to 2.5 billion, and it reached around 3 billion by 1960. In the year 2000, the global population surpassed 6 billion, and in 2012, it reached 7 billion. By 2016, the world's population was estimated to be 7.5 billion.

The United Nations (UN) estimates that by the year 2056, the global population will have reached 10 billion.

57. A dromedary is also known as a single-humped camel, in contrast to a two-humped camel. It's a myth that the humps are used by camels/dromedaries to store water. They are actually fat deposits.

Dromedaries are capable of closing their nostrils during sandstorms, which helps protect their eyes and airways from infiltrating sand.

It's accurate that dromedaries can survive for up to six months without water and food due to their efficient ability to store fat and water in their humps.

Camels are renowned for their speed over short distances and can run up to 65 km/h under such conditions. Their lifespan can extend up to 45 years.

58. In Melbourne, Australia, there is a mountain called Mount Disappointment.

It was named by two mountain climbers who were the first to reach the summit of the mountain in 1824. They had anticipated an incredibly beautiful view over the water ahead. However, the view was obstructed by trees, trees, and more trees.

59. Scientists have bred featherless chickens. By crossing regular chickens with a breed of chicken without feathers around the neck, they managed to develop this unusually unattractive breed of chickens.

The idea might have seemed fine in theory. They aimed to have chickens that could better survive in hot countries where feathered chickens couldn't handle the heat. They also intended to save money in factories, as they wouldn't need to spend time and resources removing feathers first. In theory, such a chicken wouldn't require as much food either, as nutrients wouldn't be used for feathers.

However, things didn't go so well. The roosters couldn't maintain balance during mating—they toppled off the hens.

They developed skin parasites, skin diseases, were susceptible to mosquito bites, and last but not least, they suffered from sunburn. As it turned out, they were the LEAST suitable for hot countries.

60. Six American flags were planted on the moon during the Apollo missions (Apollo 11, 12, 14, 15, 16, and 17). The flags were made of nylon. Over time, due to the intense sunlight and temperature variations, the flags have likely suffered from significant deterioration, including fading and degradation of the fabric. Some images from lunar orbiters suggest that the flags from the earlier Apollo missions, like Apollo 11, might have faded to a whitish appearance.

61. The seven wonders of the ancient world were:

The Great Pyramid of Giza: Located in Giza, it is the oldest and most famous pyramid in Egypt. It stands 139 meters tall and was built as a tomb for Pharaoh Khufu (known as Cheops in Greek). This pyramid is the only one of the seven wonders that still exists today.

Hanging Gardens of Babylon: These were terraced gardens, possibly built by King Nebuchadnezzar II around 600 BCE. However, there is uncertainty about their exact location and appearance.

Statue of Zeus at Olympia: Created by the Greek sculptor Phidias, this colossal statue of Zeus was placed in the temple at Olympia. The statue was around 13 meters tall and depicted Zeus seated on a throne. The temple was destroyed, and the statue was lost in antiquity.

Temple of Artemis at Ephesus: The Artemis Temple in Ephesus was a large and impressive Greek temple dedicated to the goddess Artemis. It was built in the 4th century BCE and was known for its size and beauty. It's worth noting that there were earlier versions of the temple on the same site.

Mausoleum at Halicarnassus: This mausoleum was built in memory of Mausolus, a Persian satrap of Caria. It was an impressive tomb constructed around 350 BCE. The mausoleum is the origin of the word "mausoleum," now commonly used to refer to large tombs.

Colossus of Rhodes: This enormous statue of the sun god Helios was erected on the island of Rhodes around 280 BCE. It stood about 32 meters tall and was one of the tallest bronze statues in antiquity. It was destroyed by an earthquake around 226 BCE.

Lighthouse of Alexandria: Also known as the Pharos Lighthouse, this monumental lighthouse was built on the island of Pharos off Alexandria, Egypt, around 280 BCE. It stood about 135 meters tall and served as an important navigational point for sailors in the Mediterranean. It was destroyed by earthquakes in the 14th century

62. The seven new wonders are:

Petra (meaning "rock"): A city in Jordan. Several tombs and temples are carved directly into the cliffs.

Machu Picchu: An Inca city in present-day Peru, located on a mountain at an altitude of 2,057 meters.

The Great Wall of China: Spanning 6,259 km plus an additional 2,233 km of natural boundaries like mountains and rivers. Construction is believed to have started around 700 BCE and continued up to the 17th century CE.

Colosseum: Completed in 80 CE. It was used for theater and gladiator battles and could accommodate 50,000 spectators.

Christ the Redeemer (Cristo Redentor): A 38-meter-tall statue of Jesus Christ. Completed in 1931, it weighs 700 tons and stands on a mountain in Rio de Janeiro, Brazil.

Chichen Itza: A Mayan city in Mexico dating back to the 6th century CE.

Taj Mahal: A white marble mausoleum near Agra, India. Completed in 1631. A legend says that the architect had his right hand cut off so he couldn't replicate the design elsewhere.

63. The first person to report strange events in the Bermuda Triangle was Christopher Columbus.

64. Christopher Columbus was born in Genoa, Italy, in 1451. His birth name in Italian was Cristoforo Colombo. He is known for his voyages across the Atlantic Ocean and his role in connecting the Old World with the New World, which had a significant impact on world history and exploration.

65. Christopher Columbus "discovered" America (which he mistakenly believed to be India) in the year 1492. Vikings discovered America in the year 1000.

Christopher Columbus's first voyage to the Americas took place in 1492, and he reached islands in the Caribbean, believing he had reached the shores of Asia (Indies). It's worth noting that Columbus's arrival marked the beginning of a period of exploration and contact between the Old World and the New World.

The Viking exploration of America, led by Leif Erikson, is believed to have occurred around the year 1000. The Norse settlement at L'Anse aux Meadows in Newfoundland, Canada, provides evidence of their presence. While the Vikings did make contact with parts of North America, their influence on the continent was limited and did not lead to significant lasting connections.

So, while both Columbus and the Vikings had interactions with the American continents, their impacts and historical contexts are different.

66. Dashrath Manjhi lived in northern India with his wife. One day, she

fell seriously ill and needed medical help. Unfortunately, the hospital was on the other side of the mountain that their village was situated near. They had to go all the way around the mountain, which took so long that his wife passed away.

Bitter over the incident, Manjhi decided to change the situation so that it wouldn't happen to others. He began single-handedly digging a tunnel through the mountain.

Over the course of two decades, he chiseled and dug until he successfully made a passage through the mountain. The tunnel is around 100 meters long and is now safe for the local community to use.

67. The names "Iceland" and "Greenland" were given by the Norse Vikings, specifically by Erik the Red, a Viking explorer and settler.

Greenland: Erik the Red, also known as Erik Thorvaldsson, was banished from Iceland for committing manslaughter and other crimes. He sailed westward and discovered a large, ice-covered landmass, which he named "Greenland" as a way to attract settlers. He hoped that the enticing name would encourage people to come and settle in this new land, despite its harsh climate. The name "Greenland" was likely a marketing tactic to make the land seem more hospitable than it actually was. The southern coastal areas of Greenland were indeed milder and more habitable compared to the interior, but the name has often been considered a bit of a misnomer.

Iceland: Iceland was discovered by Norse Viking explorers led by Hrafna-Flóki Vilgerðarson, who is said to have arrived in Iceland around 870 AD. It's believed that he gave Iceland its name based on his first winter experience. According to legend, Hrafna-Flóki climbed a mountain in winter and saw a fjord filled with drift ice, which led him to call the island "Ísland," which means "Land of Ice." The name was descriptive of the icy conditions he encountered during his initial exploration. However, it's worth noting that Iceland does have more habitable and hospitable regions, and the island's climate is not solely characterized by ice.

68. Do you know John Montagu, the 4th Earl of Sandwich? Probably not, but the sandwich is attributed to him.

He was known to enjoy playing cards. During a lengthy card game session, he became hungry but didn't want to leave the table. He also didn't want to eat food that might soil the table or his hands.

Therefore, he requested two slices of bread with meat in between. This way, he could eat and play at the same time.

Sandwich is a town east of London.

69. Lake Tahoe is the second deepest lake in the United States. It is located on the border of California and Nevada. It's a well-known and incredibly beautiful place, at least above the water's surface.

Rumor has it that there are thousands of bodies at the bottom of the lake. These include bodies thrown in by the mafia, ordinary drowning accidents, and it was a place to dispose of the bodies of deceased Chinese immigrants who died while building railroads

70. Japan experiences around 1,500 earthquakes per year.

71. There are ice hotels in Canada, Finland, Lapland, Japan, Romania, Sweden, and Switzerland. They have reception areas, bedrooms, and similar facilities. In some places, authorities require fire alarms in case any of the furnishings catch fire.

72. Zebras have stripes that function almost like fingerprints. They use these stripes to identify each other.

The stripes also make it a bit harder for predators to distinguish zebras from one another. This makes it more challenging for them to single out the weakest zebra in the herd.

73. During World War I, over 2,000 American warships were painted with zebra-like stripes. This technique was referred to as "Razzle Dazzle."

The idea behind this type of camouflage was not to make the ships invisible, but rather to make it more difficult to determine the ships' size and speed. The intention was that this would make it harder to accurately target and hit them.

74. The largest bottle size available for Champagne is called a "Nebuchadnezzar." It holds 15 liters of Champagne and is named after the biblical ruler

75. The average distance from Earth to the Moon is 384,403 kilometers. This distance increases by 3.8 centimeters per year. This phenomenon is also contributing to the lengthening of Earth's day each year.

The Earth-Moon distance change over time due to various factors, including gravitational interactions and the transfer of angular momentum. As the Moon's gravitational pull affects Earth's rotation, it causes the planet to experience a gradual slowing down of its rotation, which results in a longer day over long periods of time

76. The average distance to the Sun, however, is 149.6 million kilometers. It takes light eight minutes to travel from the Sun to Earth.

You could fit approximately 960,000 Earths inside the Sun.

77. The "Hope" diamond is a diamond that is worth 200-250 million dollars. It was intended to be sent to the Smithsonian Institution in 1958. The sender did so by mailing it through regular mail in a small box.

It was insured for $145.29.

78. WD-40 is a well-known multi-purpose product used for various applications, including lubrication, cleaning, and rust prevention. The name "WD-40" stands for "Water Displacement - 40th Attempt," signifying that it was the result of experimentation and development. It was originally created to displace water and prevent corrosion in the aerospace industry, but its versatility led to its widespread use in various fields.

79. "Broken heart syndrome" is a phenomenon where a person dies shortly after the death of a loved one, usually a spouse or partner. It is believed to be the cause of 1-3% of deaths.

80. Wild boars will consume almost anything, including urine, feces, soil, rotten meat (including human flesh), and spoiled vegetables.

Pork can still contain resistant bacteria even after cooking. The meat and fat can also readily absorb toxins, making pork more susceptible to toxins than, for example, beef.

According to Jewish scriptures (the Old Testament), they (and Muslims) are not allowed to eat pork. Perhaps that is the explanation.

81. Playing cards were invented during the Middle Ages. The four kings in the cards are believed to represent:

Spades: The biblical King David Clubs: Greek/Macedonian King Alexander the Great Hearts: French King Charlemagne Diamonds: Roman ruler Julius Caesar

82. The metric system was introduced by the French in 1795 and was designed to be logical and based on natural units.

The system was designed to be decimal-based, which made it easier to learn and use. As the metric system's use spread through Europe due to France's influence and Napoleonic conquests, other countries began to adopt it for its simplicity and ease of international trade. The system was further standardized and spread worldwide throughout the 19th and 20th centuries.

While the US signed the Treaty of the Meter in 1875, indicating an interest in the metric system, the change was never made mandatory. Americans had become accustomed to their system, which was sufficiently effective for their needs, and the cost and effort of changing to the metric system were deemed too high. Over the years, attempts have been made to metricate the US, but they have met with resistance due to the established use of the customary units in daily life, industry, and commerce.

Although the metric system is not used for most purposes in the US, it is used in science, medicine, and many sectors of industry. This dual system of measurement continues to be a distinctive feature of American life.

83. The first ballpoint pen was invented by Laszlo Biro, a Hungarian journalist, in 1938. His invention used a ball at the tip of the pen that could rotate and draw ink onto the paper, allowing for smoother and more fluid writing. This invention was a significant improvement compared to earlier writing tools, and the modern ballpoint pen has since become an essential writing technology.

84. A blue whale can reach up to 30 meters in length, weigh over 170 tons, and live between 80-90 years.

Its heart weighs as much as a car, and a human could fit inside it. Its tongue weighs nearly the same as an elephant.

They can produce deep sounds that allow them to communicate with each other at distances of up to 1,600 km.

85. The expression "Uncle Sam" was popularized during the American War of 1812. Sam Wilson, a merchant from Troy, New York, supplied food to the American army during the war. The provisions were marked with

"U.S." for United States, but the soldiers began referring to the provisions as "Uncle Sam's" to honor Sam Wilson. Over time, the expression expanded to refer to the entire USA as "Uncle Sam." It later became a popular symbol and nickname for the USA.

86. The first escalator was installed at the department store "Harrods" in London in 1878.

87. Chameleons change color depending on their mood and not based on the colors of their surroundings. It's not about camouflage.

88. Ablutophobia is the fear of washing oneself or taking a bath

89. Paraskavedekatriaphobia is the fear of Friday the 13th.

The origin of the myth about Friday the 13th is uncertain. One myth suggests it's because of Judas, who betrayed Jesus, as there were 13 people at the table.

Another myth attributes it to the Knights Templar, who were disbanded on Friday the 13th of October 1307.

People with Paraskavedekatriaphobia can actually experience heightened misfortune on Friday the 13th due to their psychological anticipation of bad luck, creating a self-fulfilling prophecy.

90. "Strategic incompetence" is a term used when someone pretends to be inept at a task with the specific goal of avoiding that task or similar tasks in the future.

This can involve intentionally making mistakes in a report, not fully cleaning the dishes, or perhaps dropping some dishes on the floor. It works best if you don't drop something every time, as that would seem suspicious to your spouse. The key is to be strategic.

91. Male mice sing to attract female mice in order to court them.

92. Mickey Mouse was originally named Mortimer Mouse. It was Walt Disney's wife's idea to change the name.

93. Nutella - one of the world's finest treats - was invented during World War II in Italy. There was a shortage of certain ingredients, including cocoa.

Pietro Ferrero had the idea to use hazelnuts as a filler to save on cocoa.

The first type of Nutella was produced in blocks, which housewives would slice and use as a spread on sometimes dry bread. However, many children would take the Nutella slice off and discard the bread.

To solve this issue, Nutella was transformed into the creamy spread we know today.

94. Unlike most other animals, the flamingo's lower jaw is fixed to the skull, while the upper jaw is not. This is why they eat with their heads upside down.

There are more plastic flamingos in the world than there are real ones.

95. There are over 50 kangaroo species.

96. Chewing gum was banned in Singapore in the 1990s due to issues related to public cleanliness and maintenance. The ban was later eased to allow the sale of therapeutic gum with medical benefits, which requires a doctor's prescription.

The fine for spitting out chewing gum or littering in Singapore is indeed quite high, as part of the government's efforts to maintain a clean environment.

Singapore does have strict laws related to public hygiene, including the requirement to flush public toilets after use. The city-state is known for its efforts to keep the environment clean and orderly.

Regarding the name "Singapore," it is believed to come from the Malay words "Singa" (lion) and "Pura" (city).

97. There is no historical evidence to conclusively prove the existence of Robin Hood. He is a legendary figure from English folklore known for being an outlaw who robbed from the rich to give to the poor. The stories of Robin Hood have been passed down through ballads, tales, and legends over the centuries, but there is no definitive historical record of a real person named Robin Hood. Instead, he remains a popular and enduring character in literature and culture.

98. Sloths are known for their slow movements and relatively inactive lifestyle. They move at an average of about two meters per minute on the ground. They are also known for sleeping a lot and can sleep up to 20 hours a day. Their slow pace and tendency to hang motionless in trees make them ideal hosts for algae, which can grow in their fur and give them a greenish color that acts as a form of camouflage.

Despite being typically slow on land, sloths are actually surprisingly good swimmers. They can swim three times faster than they can move on land, and they are also capable of holding their breath for up to 30 minutes underwater. This enables them to cross streams and rivers in their habitats.

99. A hummingbird is the only bird that can fly backwards and upside down. Its heart beats 1,000 times per minute..

100. Cats have 32 muscles in each ear, while humans have six. A cat survived a fall from the 32nd floor. The world's longest cat measured 1.2 meters in length.

A study shows that owning a cat, or having regular access to a cat, reduces the risk of heart attacks by about 30%.

101. Stars don't twinkle, it just looks that way. The light from them has to pass through the entire atmosphere, and turbulence in the atmosphere affects the light so it looks like they are twinkling

102. In 1624, Louis the 13th was the king of France. He began to lose his hair, and to hide it, he started to wear a wig. Not a discreet toupee, but large white wigs.

This started a fashion trend, not just in France, but throughout Europe. By the beginning of the 18th century, it was common for almost all European middle and upper-class men to wear wigs as a natural part of their attire.

103. A 9-month pregnancy is nothing compared to the cases of so-called "Stone babies." In this context, pregnancies lasting several decades have been reported.

The phenomenon of "Stone baby" fortunately happens rarely. It's a pregnancy outside the uterus, where the fetus dies and is so large that the body cannot break down and absorb the fetus.

Instead, the body starts to calcify the fetus, and over time, the fetus becomes petrified.

There are reports of women in developing countries who have been walking around with such a stone baby in their belly for up to about 50 years. Perhaps actually a good piece of information to give to pregnant women who complain.

104. Bob Marley is credited with popularizing reggae music worldwide. Dreadlocks, a hairstyle often associated with Marley, are a cultural and religious symbol, especially among the Rastafarian community. Maintenance of dreadlocks does involve washing; they aren't indicative of a lack of hygiene.

Bob Marley died in 1981 at the age of 36. The items mentioned in the burial are based on various reports and beliefs. Some sources suggest he was buried with a marijuana joint, a bible, and his guitar.

Bob Marley is indeed interred in a mausoleum in his birthplace of Nine Mile, in the parish of Saint Ann, Jamaica

105. Elizabeth Taylor was married a total of eight times. On average, she actually got married about every 5 years from the age of 18.

A quote from her: "If someone is foolish enough to offer me a million dollars to make a movie, I'm certainly not foolish enough to say no."

She made 50 movies and received two Oscars.

106. A study by the Library of Congress published in 2013 found that 70% of American silent feature films made from 1912 to 1929 have been completely lost, and only 14% exist in their original 35mm format.

107. Don't you like insects? Then it's good that spiders are not insects. They are called arachnids. Insects have six legs. Spiders have eight.

If you have a pathological fear of spiders, you have arachnophobia. Perhaps watch the movie of the same name.

108. Speaking of pathological fear. By the way, one can indeed die of fright. American doctors discovered this in connection with a powerful earthquake in 1994 near Los Angeles.

They reviewed the causes of death from the area. It turned out that 24 died as a result of a blood clot on that very day. This was far above the average for the area.

109. Almost 0.5% are born with an extra rib. It's not something to be envious of, as many of these people experience pain because of it.

110. Licorice Root's Medicinal Uses: Beyond its use in candy, licorice root has been utilized for thousands of years for its medicinal properties. In traditional medicine, it has been used to treat a variety of ailments ranging from digestive issues to respiratory problems. Glycyrrhizin, a compound found in licorice root, is many times sweeter than sugar and has anti-inflammatory properties. However, excessive consumption of licorice or glycyrrhizin can lead to high blood pressure, reduced potassium levels in the body, and other health issues. This is why some countries have guidelines about the consumption of licorice products, especially for pregnant women and people with certain health conditions.

111. The artist Dwight Kalb made a statue of Madonna in 1994. The statue was made of 82 kilograms of ham meat. Sounds like a delicious statue.

112. Scotland and Ireland are often cited as having the highest percentages of natural redheads in the world. The exact percentages can vary based on different sources and studies, but it's widely accepted that these two countries top the list.

Genetically, the gene responsible for red hair (the MC1R gene variant) is recessive, which means both parents must carry the gene for their child to have red hair. This gene variant is more commonly found in populations in Northern Europe, especially in the British Isles.

113. There are more pyramids in China than in Egypt. There are more pyramids in Central America than in China.

114. The founder of the whiskey brand Jack Daniels, was actually named Jasper Newton Daniel, but he was always called Jack.

He died from kicking his office safe. Normally, this safe was opened by his nephew, but one morning Jack arrived earlier than his nephew. He couldn't unlock the safe, and in anger and frustration, he kicked it hard. Jack broke his big toe. Blood poisoning set in his leg, and he died from it.

In the town where he worked, they say that the moral of the story is not to arrive too early for work.

115. In 1902, Theodore Roosevelt was the president of the USA and went on a bear hunt. Everyone else had found bears, but not Theodore.

The hunting guides then tracked down a bear that the dogs had chased and attacked. Now Theodore could shoot a bear, so they tied up the bear and fetched the president. However, the president found this unsportsmanlike, and he refused to shoot it.

Of course, the press got wind of the story, who wrote about it and made drawings of the situation with the bear the president wouldn't shoot.

Morris Michtom had a small store. After the story and drawings about Theodore and the bear, he took two teddy bears his wife had made and placed them in the window.

He named them "Teddy's bear" after the president, thus referring to the story.

The teddy bears quickly became popular and are still called teddy bears to this day.

Morris and his wife Rose Michtom subsequently founded a toy company that quickly became a great success.

116. Elephants are pregnant for two years. Their giant noses have five times more odor receptors than humans. They can smell their way to where there is water.

117. More about toys; Richard James worked as an engineer and was tasked with finding a method for stabilizing equipment on a ship using springs.

He accidentally knocked over a spring and saw how it appeared to "walk." His wife, Betty, named it "Slinky," and it became a popular toy.

James donated a lot of money, divorced his wife Betty, who continued to run the company. James then joined a religious group and traveled to Bolivia.

The Slinky is still sold to this day, but you can have mine; I don't use it anymore.

118. The torture device "Iron Maiden" was a box with spikes on the inside. A person could be placed inside the box, and when it was closed, the spikes would penetrate the person.

However, the instrument is not real and has never been used. An art collector named Matthew Peacock created such a box to demonstrate the idea of torture. But such a device has never actually been used.

119. Have you heard that carrots are supposed to be good for your eyes?

It's a myth that they are especially good for vision or eyes in general, and it's a persistent myth because it originated during World War II.

The Germans began to attack London by air. The planes carried bombs that they dropped all over London to target civilians.

The German air force was surprised that the Royal Air Force (R.A.F) often had planes in the air before the Germans even got close to London. The R.A.F could thus shoot many of them down.

The best strategy would be to surprise the English, but it seemed like the R.A.F knew the Germans' planes were coming. How could they be ready when the German planes were still so far away? How did they do it?

The Royal Air Force also had a clear advantage. They told the press and thereby the population that their pilots ate an excessive amount of carrots. They had supposedly discovered that carrots were good for the eyes, and therefore the pilots could see the Germans from a great distance.

However, it had nothing to do with carrots. They had invented an efficient radar system, but they didn't want the Germans to know about it. So, they started this myth.

120.A tongue has up to 10,000 taste buds. However, some taste buds disappear with age

121. In the 1950s, there was a company named "Frisbie Baking Co." They made pies and the like.

University students at Yale in the USA threw the round pie tins to each other while shouting "Frisbie".

Later, a plastic version came on the market as the toy "Frisbee".

122. In the 1920s, the two brothers Adolf Dassler, known as "Adi", and Rudolph Dassler started a shoe company together called "Dassler Brothers".

They fell out with each other, and Rudolph left the company to start his own.

Rudolph named his company "Puma". Adolf "Adi" renamed the old company to "Adidas".

123. A horse cannot breathe through its mouth, only through its nostrils.*Horses are obligate nasal breathers, which means they can only breathe through their nostrils. They do not breathe through their mouths due to a soft palate that blocks off the pharynx from the mouth, preventing air from moving in and out. This adaptation is believed to help prevent them from getting choked on food while running or exerting themselves.

124. The numeral system that the Western world refers to as "Arabic numerals" (0, 1, 2, 3, 4, 5, 6, 7, 8, 9) originally came from India. These numerals were introduced to Europe through translations of Arabic mathematical texts, which is why they became known as "Arabic numerals" in the West. In many parts of the Arabic-speaking world, they

are referred to as "Hindu numerals" in acknowledgment of their Indian origin.

125. Leonardo da Vinci, the renowned Renaissance polymath, is best known for his artistic works like the "Mona Lisa" and "The Last Supper." However, he was deeply interested in various scientific and mathematical subjects.

One of Leonardo's most famous illustrations, the Vitruvian Man, demonstrates the human body's proportions. This drawing embodies the ancient architect Vitruvius's ideas about the proportional relationships of the human figure, expressed in both geometrical and numerical terms.

126. The word "gymnasium" comes from Greek. The root "gymnos" does indeed mean "naked" in Greek.
Ancient Greek athletes typically trained and competed nude — a practice intended, among other things, to encourage aesthetic appreciation of the male body and as a tribute to the gods.The word "gymnasium" historically referred to a place for physical and intellectual education. The physical component of the education often involved exercise and sports, which were typically done without clothing.

127. The word "karaoke" comes from the Japanese words "kara" which means "empty" and "oke", an abbreviation of "okesutora", which means "orchestra". So, "karaoke" can be directly translated to "empty orchestra", which refers to the idea of people singing to a musical recording without

the lead vocalist.

128. Before becoming Pope Francis, Jorge Mario Bergoglio (his birth name) held a variety of jobs in his younger years, one of which was working as a bouncer at a bar in Buenos Aires, Argentina. Later, he joined the Jesuit order and began his path to priesthood and eventually became the Archbishop of Buenos Aires. In 2013, he was elected as Pope, taking the name Francis.

129. Pregnancy tests detect the presence of a hormone called human chorionic gonadotropin (hCG). While hCG is most commonly associated with pregnancy, it can also be produced by some types of testicular tumors. If a man gets a positive result on a pregnancy test, it doesn't mean he's pregnant, but it could be an early warning sign of testicular cancer. However, not all testicular cancers produce hCG, so this method should not be relied upon as a primary means of detection. It's always important to consult a medical professional for proper testing and diagnosis.

130. George W. Bush was a cheerleader during his years at Phillips Academy in Andover and also when he attended Yale University

131. George W. Bush quotes:

"You know - one of the hardest parts of my job has been to connect the Iraq war with the war on terror."

"Do you also have black people?" Said to Brazilian President Fernando Cardoso in 2001.

"I want you to know that when we talk about war, we're actually talking about peace."

"Our enemies are creative and resourceful. So are we. They never stop thinking about new ways to harm our country and our people, and neither do we."

Did you understand these statements? If so, please send me an email and explain - because I didn't.

132. In the political system of the USA, there is a "senate" and "senators". The Latin word "senatus" refers to a council of elders or advisors. "Senator" is derived from "senex," which means "old" or "elder."

133. Einstein (who was Jewish) was offered the presidency of Israel. He declined due to his belief that he lacked the necessary qualifications..

134. Diamonds are incredibly hard due to their unique atomic structure and strong carbon-carbon covalent bonds. The diamond cubic lattice arrangement of carbon atoms forms a rigid network, resulting in exceptional resistance to wear and deformation. This hardness is measured at a perfect 10 on the Mohs scale, making diamonds the hardest naturally occurring material. Their hardness finds practical use in various industries, where diamond-coated tools are employed for cutting and grinding tough materials.

135. The car brand Audi features a logo with four rings, which symbolize the amalgamation of four independent car manufacturers in 1932. These manufacturers were Audi, DKW, Horch, and Wanderer. This merger marked a significant milestone in the brand's history.

136. A safety coffin was a coffin with mechanisms that the buried person could use to sound an alarm if they were buried alive.

In 1829, a system was created in which the body had strings tied to the hands, head, and feet. These strings were connected to bells above the ground.

If the bells started ringing, the cemetery caretaker would know that a person might have been buried alive.

However, the bells often rang due to the body's natural decomposition causing movement and contractions.

137. A competition was initiated in the 19th century. The competition revolved around finding the best solution to ensure that a person is truly deceased. This was to prevent the burial of people who were still alive.

There were ideas such as pouring boiling water over the body. If there were burns or blisters, the person was not truly dead. Another idea involved igniting the nose. It was also suggested to insert a needle into the heart, with a small flag attached to the end of the needle. If the flag moved, it meant that the heart was still beating.

The winning idea was to listen for heartbeats using a device called a stethoscope.

138. In 1995, Janet Howes passed away at the age of 50. Her widower wanted to create a lasting memory of her, so he planted approximately 6,000 trees, forming a forest.

In the center of the forest, he didn't plant any trees. Instead, he created a heart-shaped clearing. When viewed from above, this heart shape is visible in the middle of the forest.

If you want to see it, you can use Google Earth. Search for: "Wickwar, South Gloucestershire, United Kingdom". Look slightly north of the town, and you will find the forest with the heart shape.

139. The artist Vincent Castiglia, who is known for creating intricate and detailed artworks using his own blood as a medium. Castiglia's works often feature themes related to life, death, and the human condition.

140. During the 18th century, the French finance minister, Etienne de Silhouette, introduced an extra tax targeting the upper class. This tax affected portraits, making them too costly for many. Consequently, there was a decline in demand for full portraits.

To address this, an alternative emerged: creating affordable black profile drawings of individuals, known as "silhouettes."

The term "silhouette" is thought to have originated from Etienne de Silhouette's name, symbolizing the economic measures associated with his tenure as a finance minister. However, the exact origin of the term remains a subject of debate.

141. Marie Curie (1867-1934), hailing from Poland, was a remarkable physicist and chemist. Her pioneering efforts in the study of radioactivity set her apart. In partnership with her husband Pierre Curie, she was awarded the Nobel Prize in Physics in 1903 for their groundbreaking work.

Marie's excellence extended further when she secured the Nobel Prize in Chemistry in 1911. This distinction marked her as the inaugural woman Nobel laureate and the first individual to claim two Nobel honors.

Additionally, she made history as the first female professor at the University of Paris.

Regrettably, it was her involvement with radioactivity that ultimately led to her demise. The full hazards of radioactivity were not yet known during that era.

142. Elizabeth Bathory (1560-1614), the Hungarian countess, has a dark reputation as one of history's most notorious female mass murderers.

She is believed to have been responsible for the deaths of numerous young girls. According to legend, her motivation for these killings was her belief that bathing in the blood of these girls could preserve her youth.

143. According to the University Medical Centre Rotterdam, which has studied 7,000 women and men, women who engage in a significant amount of domestic work live an average of three years longer than those who do not. The study reveals that men who perform the same amount of domestic work do not experience this increase in life expectancy.

So, there is absolutely no excuse for women not to learn household skills. It is, after all, for their own benefit.

By the way, it's worth mentioning that the study was conducted by a man.

144. In an otherwise ordinary forest of pine trees north of Berlin, there were around 140 larch trees.

Based on their age, they must have been planted in the 1930s. The remarkable aspect of these larch trees is that they were arranged in such a way that, when viewed from the sky, they formed a Nazi swastika.

The larch trees were most visible during autumn. Their leaves would turn yellow while the pine trees remained green.

No one knows who planted them or why. In fact, around 40 larch trees were cut down in 1995. However, the remaining larch trees propagated in the now open space, which meant that the swastika shape became visible again.

In the year 2000, the swastika formation was finally removed.

145. FIFA (Fédération Internationale de Football Association) has more member countries (211 members) than the United Nations (193 members).

146. Atacama is a desert located in Chile, and it is known for its arid conditions. The fact that 40 fossils were found there is accurate as well. These fossils, which included remains of whales, seals, and dolphins, are significant due to the desert's unexpected marine fossils.

147. On September 17, 2016, Paulo Gabriel da Silva Barros married Katyucia Lie Hoshino, both from Brazil.

Paulo is 90 cm (35.4 inches) tall and has a preference for women taller than him. His new wife, Katyucia, is 91 cm (35.8 inches) tall.

They are featured in the Guinness World Records as the world's smallest married couple.

Anna Haining Swan from Canada, who stood at 241 cm (7 feet 11 inches), married Martin van Buren Bates, who measured 236 cm (7 feet 8.98 inches). They hold the record for the tallest married couple in the world.

148. In Bolivia, there is a hotel called the "Palacio de Sal" (Salt Palace). It is a hotel constructed entirely from salt. The floors, walls, and ceiling are all made of salt, and even the furniture is crafted from salt. It is the only salt hotel in the world.

Guests are strictly prohibited from licking the walls.

149. The Aurora Ice Hotel in Alaska is a real hotel made entirely of ice, and it did face temporary closure shortly after its initial construction. The closure was reportedly due to concerns from fire authorities, who required fire safety measures such as the installation of fire alarms despite the hotel's unique material.

150. Scotland's national animal is a unicorn.

151. Fortune cookies were invented in California, specifically in the early 20th century in Japanese-American communities. The cookies were then popularized and associated with Chinese culture, often being served in Chinese restaurants. While the exact history is somewhat debated, it's widely accepted that fortune cookies have roots in California and were later embraced as part of Chinese-American culture.

152. The city of Los Angeles in the USA was originally named "El pueblo de la reina de los angeles," but was later shortened to Los Angeles

153. Before an execution of a criminal, it has been customary in most countries to offer them a last meal according to their wishes.

Lawrence Russell Brewer was one of three individuals in the United States who was convicted of the murder of James Byrd Jr.

The victim had been bound at the ankles and attached to a vehicle. He was then dragged behind the vehicle for 4-5 kilometers, resulting in his death. Lawrence Brewer was sentenced to death as a punishment and was given the opportunity to request his last meal.

He ordered two chicken-fried steaks with gravy and onions, a triple bacon cheeseburger, an omelette with cheese, beef, tomatoes, onions, peppers, and jalapenos, half a pound of barbecue meat with bread, three fajitas, a pizza, and an ice cream dessert.

However, when Brewer was served with all of this, he refused to eat anything, claiming he was not hungry.

As a result of this incident, the tradition of offering a last meal was abolished in the respective state.

154. In 2007, Philip Workman was executed. His final wish was to have a pizza donated to a random homeless person.

His request was denied by the prison, stating to the press that they do not donate to charity.

The story gained attention, and according to CNN, hundreds of citizens donated pizzas to the homeless.

155. The Nazis were the first to initiate an anti-smoking campaign.

156. The largest number of passengers on an airplane simultaneously was 1,086, which occurred in 1991 when Ethiopian Jews were fleeing Ethiopia.

However, when the plane landed, the number had increased to 1,088. Two babies were born onboard the aircraft.

157. In Japan, there are certain stores and facilities that offer the unique service of allowing individuals to try out and experience coffins before making a purchase decision. This practice is part of the Japanese culture's approach to addressing death and funeral arrangements, where individuals may want to ensure that the chosen coffin is comfortable and suits their preferences before finalizing the purchase.

158. The Empire State Building is a skyscraper with 102 floors and a height of 443 meters in New York.

In 1947, a 23-year-old woman committed suicide by jumping from the building.

She landed on top of a limousine and died instantly. LIFE magazine captured the photograph, published it, and titled it "The Most Beautiful Suicide."

159. In 1914, a train traveled from Grangeville to Lewiston in the state of Idaho. The train carried passengers and mail, as usual. Among the passengers was 5-year-old Charlotte Pierstorff, who was traveling from her parents to her grandparents. She got off the train and was escorted to her grandparents' home by an adult. This wasn't a problem until authorities found out about it.

In modern times, it might be considered illegal to allow a 5-year-old to travel alone, but in 1914, it wasn't uncommon. A regular passenger ticket would have been too expensive for the family, and sneaking their daughter aboard as a stowaway wouldn't have been a viable solution either.

Necessity is the mother of invention, as they say, and the resourceful parents came up with a solution that actually worked.

The parents bought some stamps, affixed them to their daughter's coat, and sent her not as a passenger, but as a parcel through the mail.

The postal system had the obligation to deliver any - and I mean any - package through the mail. Regulations on packages weren't as strict back then. So, she had to sit in the mail train car, but that wouldn't be a problem considering the short duration of the trip.

Not only did they save a lot of money, but the postal service also had the duty to deliver packages directly to people's doors. Consequently, daughter Charlotte was safely escorted right to her grandparents' doorstep and handed over to them.

160. Eating the liver of certain animals, including dogs, can be dangerous due to the high levels of vitamin A. Vitamin A toxicity, also known as hypervitaminosis A, can occur when excessive amounts of vitamin A are consumed. Animal livers, including dog livers, are known to contain very high levels of vitamin A, which can lead to symptoms such as

nausea, vomiting, headache, dizziness, and in severe cases, even death. It's important to be cautious about consuming animal l

161. Winston Churchill said:

"I am ready to meet my Maker. Whether my Maker is prepared for the great ordeal of meeting me is another matter."

"The best argument against democracy is a five-minute conversation with the average voter."

"A politician needs the ability to foretell what is going to happen tomorrow, next week, next month, and next year. And to have the ability afterwards to explain why it didn't happen."

"Success is not final, failure is not fatal: It is the courage to continue that counts."

162. In most places in Europe, you can get away with a few thousand kroner in fines if you drive too fast.

In Finland, they have a different system. Here, you have to pay speeding fines based on your income.

In 2001, Anssi Vanjoki had to pay around 116,000 euros for speeding in a residential area. This amounted to 14 days' worth of salary.

163. In Earth's orbit, there is a satellite named LAGEOS 1 that NASA has launched. This satellite carries a plaque designed by Carl Sagan.

The plaque depicts a map of Earth, showing how the continents looked at the time of the satellite's launch.

The satellite is estimated to exist for about eight million years, and the intention is that whoever finds the plaque can calculate when the plaque was launched by observing the continents' positions on the map.

One might think that NASA could simply write a date on the plaque.

164. In the Middle Ages, it was legally binding to be engaged. If you had promised to marry a woman, you were obligated to follow through. Breaking the engagement was treated like breaching a written contract, and you could be sued.

Later on, this legal obligation was removed, and in most places around the world, being engaged is not legally binding. The commercial world introduced a new tradition: the engagement ring. The idea was that if the man broke the agreement - the engagement - the woman was entitled to keep the ring.

165. Almonds are fruit, not nuts.

166. Buzz Aldrin was the second person to walk on the Moon during the Apollo 11 mission in 1969. His mother's name was Marion Moon, and his connection to space exploration was coincidentally reflected in her surname.

In September 2002, Buzz Aldrin was confronted by conspiracy theorist Bart Sibrel, who confronted him with aggressive questions about the Moon landing's authenticity. The confrontation escalated, and Aldrin did punch Sibrel after being provoked.

After returning from the Moon, Buzz Aldrin did face personal challenges, including depression and alcoholism. He has been open about his struggles and has worked to raise awareness about mental health issues. Aldrin has been married and divorced three times, reflecting the personal difficulties he faced following his historic journey to the Moon.

167. There are 2 golf balls on the Moon. Alan Shepard brought them along with a golf club. It took him 3 attempts to hit the first one, which is likely challenging while wearing a bulky spacesuit.

168. It is scientifically proven that women appear more attractive after a few drinks. The concept of "beer goggles" is a colloquial term used to describe the phenomenon where alcohol consumption can lower

inhibitions and alter one's perception of attractiveness. While alcohol can indeed affect perception and judgment, it's important to clarify some details.

Alcohol's impact on perception is not limited to women becoming "more attractive." Alcohol can impair judgment and affect the way people perceive others, including their physical appearance. It can lead to an overestimation of attractiveness or a tendency to overlook physical flaws. However, this effect is not solely tied to women and can apply to both genders.

The concept of symmetry and attractiveness is rooted in studies showing that people tend to find symmetrical faces more appealing. While alcohol can influence one's ability to perceive facial symmetry, the term "beer goggles" is more of a colloquial expression than a scientific term.

169. 1816 was known as the "Year Without a Summer."

In April 1815, Mount Tambora erupted on the island of Sumbawa in Indonesia, resulting in one of the most massive volcanic eruptions in history.

Gases, dust, and ash were propelled into the atmosphere, which over the next 18 months spread across much of the northern hemisphere.

The Earth experienced cooling as reduced sunlight reached the surface due to the ash and the formation of more clouds. This led to poor harvests, causing disease and death.

Similarly, in the years 535 and 536, the climate was extremely abnormal. There was unusual snowfall in Syria during the summer, and sunlight was weak with only a few hours of daylight. Poor harvests resulted from the cold temperatures and limited sunlight.

While the exact cause is not definitively known, these climate anomalies are believed to have been triggered by volcanic eruptions.

170. "Karate" is a Japanese martial art that translates to "empty hand." The term reflects the fact that karate practitioners primarily use their hands, feet, and body for striking and defense, without the need for weapons. "Kara" means "empty," and "te" means "hand." Karate emphasizes physical and mental discipline, self-defense techniques, and the development of character. It originated in Okinawa and has become a popular martial art and form of physical training practiced worldwide.

171. Lobsters harbor bacteria in their meat, some of which can pose a threat to human health. These bacteria undergo rapid multiplication when the lobster perishes.

As a precaution against potential foodborne illnesses, the practice of boiling lobsters alive is advocated, aiming to reduce the risk.

172. Lightning is a discharge of electricity that occurs within a thunderstorm. It can travel between clouds, from cloud to ground, or even from ground to cloud. The process involves the movement of charged particles, and the resulting rapid expansion of air due to intense heat generates shockwaves that we perceive as thunder. Globally, there are more than a billion lightning strikes each year, contributing to the awe-inspiring natural phenomenon of thunderstorms.

173. William Herschel, a prominent astronomer, is known for his contributions to the study of the solar system and the universe. He speculated that the sun and the moon might be potentially habitable worlds.

William Henry Pickering, another astronomer, proposed the idea that the moon might have swarms of insects or other forms of life.

174. The Soviet Union conducted a scientific drilling project known as the Kola Superdeep Borehole during the 1970s and 1980s. The purpose of the project was to study the Earth's crust and gain insights into its composition and structure at great depths. The Kola Superdeep Borehole reached a depth of 12,262 meters (about 7.5 miles), making it the deepest artificial point on Earth's surface. The project yielded valuable geological and scientific data, contributing to our understanding of the Earth's crust and subsurface conditions.

175. The Sveriges Riksbank, the central bank of Sweden, is recognized as the world's first central bank to issue banknotes. In 1661, the bank began issuing handwritten notes as a form of currency. This innovation marked a shift from using coins as the primary medium of exchange. The concept of banknotes eventually spread to other parts of Europe and around the world, playing a significant role in modern monetary systems.

176. The act of proposing a toast by raising and clinking glasses is believed to have its origins in ancient rituals and practices. In various cultures, people would raise cups or bowls filled with liquids, such as wine, in honor of gods, spirits, or deceased individuals. This act was often accompanied by spoken words or prayers to pay homage or seek blessings. The practice has persisted through time, evolving into the modern tradition of toasting, where people raise their glasses to celebrate, express good wishes, or commemorate special occasions. The ancient Greeks and Romans, among other civilizations, engaged in similar libation rituals as part of their religious and social customs.

177. In 1939, Lothrop Withington, a Harvard University student, organized a competition where participants would swallow live goldfish. Withington himself won the competition and the prize money of $10. This event was part of a series of eccentric contests that took place at various universities during that time.

The trend of swallowing live goldfish became a fad on college campuses, with participants attempting to break each other's records. The notion of the competition escalating to the point where participants attempted to swallow multiple goldfish is also accurate, and it was one of the more extreme examples of strange and sometimes harmful fads that emerged during that era.

178. The saying "the grass is always greener on the other side" is often used metaphorically to express the idea that people tend to perceive others' situations as better than their own. However, in the literal sense, the color of grass can be influenced by various factors, such as the type of grass, weather conditions, maintenance, and more.

The optical illusion described in the statement is related to how we perceive color and texture. When you view grass from a different angle or distance, the lighting and visual perspective can create the illusion that it appears greener or more lush compared to when you're looking directly down at your own grass. Additionally, the proximity to the grass you're observing can affect how clearly you see the individual blades and the underlying ground.

179. M&Ms, created by Forrest Mars and Bruce Murrie, were designed with a hard candy shell to prevent melting and were initially intended for military rations due to their durability. In "E.T. the Extra-Terrestrial," the plan was to use M&Ms to lure E.T., but the makers of the candy did not give permission for its use. As a result, Reese's Pieces, a competitor's product, was used instead, and this decision led to a significant boost in sales for Reese's Pieces.

This instance marked one of the early examples of product placement in movies and TV shows, a practice that has become common in the entertainment industry. The chocolate bar "Snickers" is indeed named after a horse owned by Forrest Mars, combining his love for horses with the candy business.

180. In 1912, an event known as "Loterie de Bébés" or "Baby Lottery" toke place in Paris, France. The purpose of this event was indeed to raise funds for a charitable cause, particularly a hospital, and to find homes for orphaned or abandoned children. The concept involved purchasing tickets, and the winners were not awarded monetary prizes but rather the opportunity to adopt a child.

The Baby Lottery was organized with the intention of combining fundraising with social welfare efforts, providing financial support to a hospital while also addressing the needs of orphaned or abandoned infants. The event is an example of an unconventional fundraising approach that aimed to address societal issues during that time.

181. Many smartphones have a shutter sound that plays when taking photos, and this sound can often be customized or turned off. However, in Japan, due to concerns related to privacy and illicit photography, some mobile phone regulations have been introduced. These regulations aim to prevent surreptitious photography, such as upskirting or taking unauthorized photos without the subject's knowledge or consent.

In Japan, the shutter sound on smartphones is typically mandatory and cannot be silenced to discourage intrusive photography. This practice is intended to protect privacy and deter inappropriate photography. The term "upskirting" refers to the act of taking pictures up someone's skirt without their consent, which is considered a violation of privacy and has led to legal and societal concerns.

182. On January 15, 1919, a large molasses tank owned by the Purity Distilling Company burst in Boston's North End neighborhood. The rupture released an enormous wave of molasses, estimated to have been about 8 to 15 feet high, which rushed through the streets at speeds of up to 35 miles per hour (56 km/h). This caused extensive damage to buildings, homes, and vehicles, and tragically resulted in the deaths of 21 people and injuries to many more.

The incident is known as the Great Molasses Flood or the Boston Molasses Disaster. The explosion was attributed to a combination of factors, including warmer-than-usual temperatures that caused the molasses to ferment and generate gases, which built up pressure inside the tank. The tank's structural weaknesses contributed to its failure.

The aftermath of the molasses flood was significant, with the area affected taking years to clean up and recover. The story of the disaster has become a part of Boston's history and is often used to illustrate the potential dangers of poorly designed industrial structures and negligence in safety precautions.

183. While it is often said that no two snowflakes are alike, this assertion is not entirely accurate. Snowflakes form when water vapor freezes in unique crystalline structures. The intricate patterns of snowflakes are indeed incredibly diverse and can vary based on factors such as temperature, humidity, and atmospheric conditions.

However, on a molecular level, the basic building blocks of snowflakes are water molecules, and the fundamental structure of these molecules remains the same. This means that while the specific patterns and shapes of snowflakes can vary significantly, there is a finite range of possible molecular arrangements, and it is theoretically possible for two snowflakes to be very similar or even identical in structure.

184. In ancient times, suicide was considered illegal. Legally, the punishment for suicide was public humiliation, and one's possessions were confiscated by authorities, preventing any inheritance for the surviving family members. Priests also refused to grant forgiveness for the act.

For individuals who wished to end their lives, an alternative method emerged. They would commit murder, ensuring their execution by the authorities.

This practice often targeted children, particularly orphans. An individual would find such a child, commit murder, and then inform the authorities of the act. As a result, they would receive the death penalty, but before their execution, they could obtain absolution from a priest.

185. Dagmar Overby was a Danish serial killer known as the "Angel Maker." She committed between 8 and 25 child murders from 1911 to 1920.

She placed advertisements in newspapers offering to help young women who had found themselves in difficult situations. These women had become pregnant outside of marriage, which was a significant issue at that time.

Young women would approach Dagmar, who claimed she could arrange adoptions for the babies with childless couples. She promised that the child would grow up in a relatively affluent family and have a good life. In return for her services, Dagmar charged a fee to the young women.

After receiving the babies and their payment, Dagmar would kill the infants and burn their bodies in her stove.

The case garnered significant attention across the country and led to Denmark enacting laws regarding foster children and supervision of children born out of wedlock

186. The founder of the Mormon Church, Joseph Smith, had certain racial teachings, including the belief in a curse on some individuals. According to some accounts, he taught that black people were descended from Cain and were cursed with a darker skin as a sign of that curse. However, it's important to note that these teachings have been disavowed

by the modern-day Church of Jesus Christ of Latter-day Saints (LDS Church), which is the main body of the Mormon faith.

In 1978, the LDS Church, under the leadership of President Spencer W. Kimball, announced a revelation that extended full priesthood and temple blessings to all worthy male members, regardless of their race or lineage. This change marked a significant shift in the church's stance on race.

Mormon theology has a doctrine of "eternal progression." This doctrine suggests that individuals can become gods in the afterlife, following the example of God the Father.

187. The Louvre originally started as a medieval fortress built in the 12th century to defend against Viking raids and other threats. Over the centuries, it underwent various transformations and expansions. It was later turned into a royal palace by French kings and eventually became a museum during the French Revolution. The Louvre is one of the world's largest and most visited museums today.

188. The first barcode was scanned on a pack of Wrigley's chewing gum in 1974. Barcodes and barcode scanners have since become a fundamental part of the retail and logistics industries for tracking and managing products. The scanners read the variations in the widths of the lines, not the spaces between them, to decode the information stored in the barcode.

189. Edvardo Ribas was a radio host in the 1940s. He was critical of politicians and expressed his political views in his radio speeches.

He decided to commit suicide as a political act and planned to do it publicly during his broadcast time.

He delivered his final political speech on the radio and shot himself in the abdomen so that all listeners could hear it.

However, there were misunderstandings between him and the technician, so when he shot himself, his speech was interrupted by commercials.

190. Between 50% and 80% of the solid matter in feces consists of bacteria that have resided in the intestines. The remaining components include water, deceased cells, and undigested remnants of food. In recent years, researchers have explored and tested a procedure known as fecal microbiota transplantation (FMT). This involves collecting fecal material from healthy individuals and introducing it into the intestines of people with conditions like poor digestion. It's worth noting that FMT is a medically recognized approach used to address specific gastrointestinal disorders.

191. There are people who work in Gastroenterology. Such gastroenterologists have found through controlled experiments that individuals produce between 500 and 1,500 milliliters of intestinal gas per day. Now you might not be so unhappy with your job anymore?

These small explosions occur because bacteria digest food in our intestines and release gas.

192. Coffee is the second most sold product after oil. Coffee contains a significant amount of antioxidants. Research indicates that coffee consumption can reduce the risk of prostate cancer.

More than two billion cups of coffee are consumed daily worldwide. In Brazil, over five million people are involved in the cultivation and harvesting of coffee beans.

Finland holds the record for being the country with the highest coffee consumption.

193. 91-year-old Kurt Jarant died of old age. His wife and daughter were stopped at the security checkpoint when they attempted to fly from England to Berlin with him.

They had placed him in a wheelchair and claimed he was asleep. However, the security personnel didn't believe it, and it was later discovered that he had been deceased for at least 12 hours.

194. In the 1950s, G. Clifford Jr. was the president/chairman of the "Society for Indecency to Naked Animals," which can be translated as the

"Association Against Indecency to Naked Animals." This was, of course, in the United States.

The purpose of the association was to advocate for legislation requiring animals to be partially clothed when in public spaces.

The association claimed to have over 50,000 members and followers in England, the USA, and Canada.

However, it turned out to be a prank orchestrated by two comedians.

195. Some species of turtles, such as the Fitzroy River turtle, have the ability to absorb oxygen through their cloaca, which is a multi-purpose opening used for excretion and reproduction. This adaptation allows them to extract oxygen from water, particularly in oxygen-depleted environments, and is a unique respiratory adaptation among turtles.

196. Horse racing has been popular for a long time. In 1923, Frank Hayes won a race in New York. He was riding a horse named "Sweet Kiss."

It was the first time he had won a race. Judges approached him to congratulate him, but they discovered that Frank had passed away. He had suffered a heart attack.

197. Here's a recipe from Sardinia, Italy for making the cheese Casu Marzu:

Ingredients:

1. Pecorino Sardo cheese

Instructions:

- Start by taking a wheel of Pecorino Sardo cheese.
- Place the cheese outside, uncovered.
- Cheese flies will lay their eggs in the cheese. Allow these eggs to hatch into 8mm-long larvae (maggots).
- The larvae will consume parts of the cheese, causing it to ferment and some of the cheese to become soft and liquid. The liquid part of the cheese is called "lagrima."
- The cheese can be eaten with or without the larvae. It's apparently considered courageous to eat it with the larvae.
- Serve the cheese with bread and red wine.

198. The total length of all the blood vessels in the human body is estimated to be around 60,000 miles (approximately 97,000 kilometers)

199. The function of the human appendix (blindtarmen) has been a subject of debate among researchers and medical professionals. While it was historically believed to have no function and was considered a

vestigial organ, more recent research suggests that it may play a role in the immune system and the maintenance of gut bacteria.

200. Flies spread more bacteria than, for example, cockroaches. Flies, for instance, are attracted to rotten meat and feces. They cannot chew their food, but instead ingest it and then regurgitate it along with enzymes that break down the food.

While they feed on the rotten meat or feces, they naturally stand on it with their feet, which become filled with bacteria. Afterward, they immediately fly over to your cake and land on it. Enjoy your meal.

201. The record for the longest speech is held by Fidel Castro.The speech, which lasted 4 hours and 29 minutes, began with Fidel saying that he would be brief.

202. A piece of A4 paper cannot be folded more than 7 times.

203. The modern umbrella, as we know it today, evolved over time with contributions from different inventors and cultures. However, one notable figure often associated with the development of the modern umbrella is Jonas Hanway, an Englishman. In the mid-18th century, around the 1750s, Jonas Hanway is credited with popularizing the use of umbrellas in England.

Hanway was known for using umbrellas as a means to protect himself from the rain, and he faced initial ridicule and criticism for doing so. Nevertheless, his persistence in using and advocating for umbrellas helped contribute to their acceptance and usage as rain protection tools.

204. On Oprah Winfrey's birth certificate, her name is actually listed as "Orpah," not "Oprah." She was named after a biblical figure named Orpah. Due to consistent mispronunciation, Winfrey opted to use the name "Oprah" instead.

205. The total amount of salt in the Earth's oceans is estimated to be around 50 million billion tons (50 quintillion tons). If this salt were spread evenly over the entire surface area of the Earth, including both land and water, it would create a layer of salt only about 44 meters thick

206. Hitler had a personal physician, Dr. Theodor Morell. Dr. Morell administered injections of cocaine and amphetamine to Hitler. At that time, the negative effects of these substances were not well understood, including their impact on personality and judgment.

Amphetamine has been accused of potentially causing conditions like Parkinson's disease. A disease that Hitler likely had in his final days.

Theodor Morell was not punished for anything after the end of the war. He died from obesity in 1948.

207. Adolf Hitler had two sisters named Angela and Paula, as well as a brother named Alois Hitler Jr. Angela, Paula, and Alois Jr. are known siblings of Hitler. While there are still some living descendants of Adolf Hitler's family, they have distanced themselves from his legacy and strive to maintain privacy.

208. There are thousands of chemicals in cigarettes, with 43 of them known to be carcinogenic.

Some of the chemicals present in cigarette smoke include:

- Acetone: Also used as nail polish remover.
- Arsenic: Sometimes used as rat poison.
- Formaldehyde: Used for preservation and disinfection.
- Toluene: Used in making paints.
- Methanol: Also known as wood alcohol, used as antifreeze.

According to the World Health Organization (WHO), tobacco kills up to half of its users, with six million deaths annually worldwide due to tobacco. Around five million of these deaths are direct smokers, and the rest are due to secondhand smoke.

It is believed that over 100 million people died from tobacco-related causes in the 20th century. This number exceeds the combined casualties of both World War I and World War II.

209. The average height of Roman soldiers during the time of the Roman Empire is estimated to have been around 165-170 cm (5'5"-5'7"), which is shorter compared to modern average heights. This information is supported by historical records and archaeological findings.

210. The Wright brothers, Orville and Wilbur Wright, successfully flew the first powered aircraft on December 17, 1903. The Japanese attack on Pearl Harbor occurred on December 7, 1941. The Apollo 11 mission, which successfully landed humans on the moon, took place on July 20, 1969.

211. The pharmaceutical industry spends more money on marketing than on research

212. Turritopsis dohrnii, commonly known as the "immortal jellyfish," is a species of jellyfish that has gained attention due to its unique ability to revert back to an earlier life stage after reaching maturity. This process, known as transdifferentiation, allows the jellyfish to potentially escape death and potentially live indefinitely. While it is often referred to as "immortal," it's important to note that the concept of true immortality is complex and not fully understood.

213. Modern smartphones have significantly more computing power than the computers used by NASA during the Apollo missions to the Moon in 1969. The computing technology available at that time was much less advanced compared to today's standards, and the computers used for space travel were large and had limited processing capabilities. In contrast, smartphones today are highly sophisticated and can perform complex tasks with much greater speed and efficiency.

214. The Irish Potato Famine, also known as the Great Famine, occurred in the mid-19th century (1845-1852) and led to a significant decrease in Ireland's population due to mass emigration and death caused by famine and disease. The population of Ireland today is lower than it was before the potato famine

215. The book titled "Everything Men Know About Women" by Dr. Alan Francis is known for having 120 blank pages. The humor in the book comes from the idea that men are often portrayed as not understanding women, and the blank pages play on that theme. The book was published as a humorous novelty item.

216. The use of paper money originated in China. The earliest recorded use of paper money dates back to the Tang Dynasty (618–907 AD) in China. However, it was during the Song Dynasty (960–1279 AD) that paper money became more widely adopted as a means of exchange. The Chinese government at that time issued official paper currency backed by the state. The concept of paper money eventually spread to other parts of the

world, influencing the development of modern banking and monetary systems.

217. Google is actively researching artificial intelligence. Their system can now lip-read better than humans can. So be cautious if you have a camera in your computer screen.

In fact, the director of the FBI has recommended covering the camera, possibly with dark tape. However, not due to Google, but because many hackers can activate it and thus see everything you do.

218. In 2014, there were reports about Hawaii considering offering homeless individuals one-way plane tickets to leave the state as a part of an effort to address the homelessness issue. This approach was met with mixed reactions and criticisms.

219. The term "hipster" originated in the 1940s to refer to fans of jazz music and the associated subculture. The term has evolved over the years and has been used to describe various cultural movements and styles. While the original context may have been related to jazz fans, the term has taken on new meanings and associations in modern times.

220. Bill Gates' wealth at one point was 4-5 times higher than North Korea's GDP.

221. In Hong Kong in 2012, there was a father who offered 65 million dollars to the man who could get his lesbian daughter to marry him.

222. Orthodox Jews are not allowed to use electronics on the Sabbath (Friday). This means they cannot turn lights on and off or use a phone. They cannot open the refrigerator as it would turn on the light.

Therefore, they also cannot use a regular elevator on the Sabbath because it requires pressing the button to select the desired floor. After that, they would need to press another button to exit the elevator on the desired floor. This is not permissible.

A "Sabbath elevator" is designed for this purpose. It automatically stops and opens its doors at every floor.

223. When a woman has her first child, her brain's structure undergoes changes and grows.

Different areas of the brain expand, including a part known as "gray matter." This region of the brain is associated with emotions, but what might be more intriguing is that it's also linked to judgment and reasoning.

Does this shed light on certain behaviors?

224. The day after Donald Trump won the election as the President of the United States, the most used "how did..." search on Google was: "how did Trump win."

225. In the mid-19th century, so-called "freak shows" became popular. These were exhibitions of people with deformities. One of the most well-known of these "curiosities" was Joseph Merrick, who had a range of genetic abnormalities that caused deformities on his skin and bones. He was called the Elephant Man because his mother believed Joseph acquired these conditions when she was scared by an elephant while pregnant.

The Bearded Lady was named Annie Jones. Due to a growth disorder, she had a mustache when she was five years old.

The Hottentot Venus was from the Khoikhoi people in South Africa and had what was considered the largest buttocks of her time, which was put on display. She was first taken to England and participated in these freak shows. In 1814, she was sold into slavery and went to France. There, she was treated like an animal, and several so-called "scientists" used her as "evidence" that Africans were more animalistic than other races. She could speak four different languages, by the way. How many do you speak?

Due to her mistreatment and being forced into prostitution, she died at the age of 25 from alcohol and disease. Her skeleton, brain, and genitals were put on display in museums, where they were exhibited until 1974.

226. The colors of the Olympic rings are: blue, yellow, black, green, and red. The reason for these colors is that at least one of these colors appears in every national flag.

227. Martin Luther's views on Jews evolved over his lifetime. In his earlier writings, Luther expressed hope for their conversion to Christianity and criticized the Catholic Church's treatment of Jews. However, as he grew older, his views became increasingly negative and anti-Semitic. In his later works, like "On the Jews and Their Lies," Luther condemned Jews and advocated for harsh measures against them, including expulsion and burning of their synagogues. It's important to acknowledge this aspect of his legacy while also recognizing his broader contributions to theology and the Reformation movement.

228. Anablephobia is a fear of looking upwards.

229. Kaprofagia refers to the urge to consume feces.

In a disturbing incident, a man sneaked into the women's restroom at a shopping center in China and startled women before they could flush their waste down the toilet. He proceeded to consume their feces.

230. Are you superstitious? You might believe that walking under a ladder brings bad luck. But where does this idea originally come from?

This notion has its origins in Egypt, but here, ladders were actually seen as a symbol of luck. They have been found in burial sites and likely symbolized the idea of climbing up to the gods.

The ancient Egyptians worshiped triads of gods, meaning gods that were three gods in one, and a ladder placed against a wall depicted a triangle - a trinity.

If an ordinary person walked under a ladder, it would be considered an insulting action towards the gods. It was like stepping into their domain. The gods would then become displeased with the person and bring them misfortune.

Egypt was conquered by the Romans, who often adopted foreign gods and customs, including this idea.

231. Vatican City is the world's smallest country, covering approximately 0.44 square kilometers. It issues citizenship like other countries, and there are about 600 citizens of Vatican City. Most of them reside outside the country. Their top-level domain is ".va".

The country is named after the Vatican Hill on which it is situated.

232. In the old days, women used to wear black dresses only when they became widows, and they would wear nothing else for two years as a sign of mourning. Queen Victoria wore black mourning attire for 40 years after the death of Prince Albert.

233. The head of the Catholic Church is titled "pope." The word "pope" comes from Latin "papa," which in turn derives from the Greek word "pappas."

The word means "father." The papal title, therefore, means "father," despite the fact that in the Bible, in Matthew chapter 23 verse 9, it is stated not to call anyone "father" as a title. But perhaps the pope was absent when they discussed this in Bible school.

234. Suicide was considered a criminal offense in England until the Suicide Act 1961 decriminalized the act of suicide and the attempt to commit suicide in the UK. Prior to that, attempting suicide could indeed lead to legal repercussions, including imprisonment.

235. In 1960, the CIA tried a spy program that involved a cat.

A battery, a microphone, and an antenna were implanted along the cat's tail.

The spy cat was intended for surveillance purposes, but when it was released, it ran in front of a taxi and was killed.

236. In 1995, a patent was approved. It has the patent number "US5443036". It's a method for exercising your cat. The idea is to use a laser pointer. The patent expired in 2007.

237. In Europe, between 50-60 million Christmas trees are harvested every year.

238. Ancient Hindus in India had a method to determine whether people were telling a lie or not.

They would chew on a mouthful of rice and then spit it out. The idea was that if someone was lying, they would have a dry mouth, which would be evident from the rice.

239. Swimming is healthy, but some people experience irritated eyes when being in a public swimming pool.

In the past, it was thought to be due to chlorine in the water, but it appears to be because of chemical structures containing nitrogen - such as those also found in sweat and urine - combined with chlorine.

240. The length of the line that can be drawn by an average pencil depends on factors such as the hardness of the pencil lead and how much pressure is applied while drawing. However, it's widely accepted that a typical pencil with standard graphite lead can draw a line around 50 kilometers long.

241. Ilse Koch was called the "Witch of Buchenwald." She was married to Otto Koch, a commandant of the Buchenwald concentration camp.

She enjoyed walking around and randomly whipping prisoners, and she became known for having prisoners with tattoos killed.

The skin was then used to make lampshades. Ilse committed suicide in prison in 1967.

242. The popular notion that goldfish have a memory span of only a few seconds is a misconception. Scientific studies have demonstrated that goldfish have a memory that can last for several months, and they are capable of learning and retaining information such as recognizing colors, shapes, and even basic conditioning responses. While their memory might not be as advanced as some other animals, it is far from being limited to

just a few seconds.

243. The Bible does not say that three holy kings visited Jesus shortly after his birth. Some people from the East came to worship him. In reality, these visitors were astrologers or stargazers.

Jesus was not an only child. After Jesus, Mary had more children.

244. Harry S Truman served as the 33rd President of the United States. The "S" in his name doesn't stand for a specific name; it was chosen as a compromise between his two grandfathers, Anderson Shipp Truman and Solomon Young. The "S" itself is not an abbreviation for any particular name.

245. The Japanese soldier Hiroo Onoda roamed around in the Philippine jungle for 29 years. He was a soldier in World War II and either did not know or refused to believe that the war had ended. He hid in the jungle with four other soldiers and continued to engage in guerrilla actions.

One of the soldiers "surrendered" in 1950, another was shot in 1954, while the third was killed by the police during a guerrilla action in 1972.

Onoda emerged in 1974 and formally surrendered to the Philippine president. He died in Japan in 2014.

246. The most well-known and investigated religious artifact in the world is the "Shroud of Turin." It is a long piece of fabric with an image of a man, which many believe to be an image of Jesus. Various scientific studies have been conducted. Some researchers believe it is from the 12th or 13th century, the medieval period, while others believe it dates back to between 280 BCE and 220 CE. It's difficult to reach a scientific conclusion due to its movement and handling over time, which has led to contamination from different eras on the shroud.

The Shroud is located in Turin, Italy. In 2015, it was exhibited to the public, and over two million people visited the site in about two months.

Science cannot explain how the markings on the Shroud could have originated or been applied. The imprint clearly shows a human figure with a narrow face, beard, long hair down to the shoulders, and wounds around the head and hands. Many people believe it depicts Jesus. As a closing note, I'd like to mention that I found several passages in the Bible related to men's hair that might be worth considering when forming your beliefs about this cloth:

Ezekiel chapter 44, verse 20: "They shall not shave their heads or let their locks grow long; they shall surely trim the hair of their heads." First Corinthians chapter 11, verse 14: "Does not nature itself teach you that if a man wears long hair, it is a disgrace for him?"

247. Approximately 35% of the world's countries drive on the "wrong" side of the road - meaning the left side. The countries where left-side driving is still practiced often have historical connections to English rule.

The reason for left-side driving is rooted in history and is related to the practice of horseback riding. In the past, it was easier for right-handed individuals to mount and dismount a horse from the left side. This was especially important when many people carried a long knife or sword on their left side. Mounting from the left allowed them to swing their right leg over the horse more easily.

Riding on the left side was common, but peasants and others of lower status were required to ride on the right side to avoid obstructing and impeding the path of aristocrats, who could ride faster. This might be why Napoleon mandated right-side riding in France and the countries he conquered.

In America, after the Revolution and gaining independence from England, they did not want to follow the same practice as the British, so they adopted right-side driving.

248. Mexico City is one of the world's largest cities. The city was founded by the Aztecs and was called Tenochtitlan. It now has around 20 million residents. This is causing the city to sink.

The underground cannot withstand the pressure, and residents are draining the groundwater. This is causing significant parts of the city to sink.

Other sinking cities include New York, Houston, Venice, Shanghai, and Bangkok.

249. Jeff Bezos, who founded the IT company Amazon in 1994, initially wanted to name the company "Cadabra."

Later, he came up with the name "Amazon" to indicate its vastness and to ensure it appeared among the first in internet searches at that time.

250. LEGO, a globally recognized brand of interlocking toy bricks, was founded by Ole Kirk Christiansen in 1932 in Billund, Denmark. The name "LEGO" is derived from the Danish words "leg godt," which mean "play well." Initially, the company produced wooden toys, and it wasn't until 1949 that they began manufacturing the now-iconic plastic interlocking bricks that we know today.

251. Google was created by Larry Page and Sergey Brin. Larry began developing the search engine in 1996 and initially called it "Backrub." Later, it was changed to Google, derived from the term "googol," which represents the number 1 followed by 100 zeros.

In 1997, Larry Page tried to sell the search engine to another search engine called "Excite" for a price of $1,600,000, but the deal was not completed.

Today, Google is valued at over $500 billion. "Excite" is not used much today – do you use it?

252. On Hollywood's "Walk of Fame," celebrities can receive a star with their name on the sidewalk.

Donald Duck, Mickey Mouse, Shrek, and Kermit all have stars on Hollywood's "Walk of Fame."

253. In some states in the USA, it is legal to have chimpanzees as pets.

Sandra Herold had a chimpanzee that she adopted in 1995 when he was very young. She named him Travis.

Travis was raised as a child. He slept in the same bed as Sandra, wore human clothes, ate at the table, and drank from wine glasses.

Fourteen years later, in 2009, he had grown significantly and suddenly attacked Sandra's friend Charla Nash. Travis bit off both of Charla's hands, most of her face, and left her blind. Travis was killed.

254. Hans Steininger possessed an exceptionally long beard in the 16th century. It's reported that during a fire incident in his city, he tripped over his long beard, fell, and suffered fatal injuries. This incident is often cited as a cautionary tale about the potential hazards of extreme facial hair. While the details might vary slightly in different accounts, the core elements of the story are consistent, making it a well-known historical anecdote.

255. Several studies and investigations have found that the tray tables on airplanes can indeed harbor more germs and bacteria than the toilet seats. This is often attributed to the frequency of cleaning and disinfecting different parts of the aircraft. While the cleanliness can vary between airlines and flights, it's widely recognized that tray tables can be a hotspot for germs due to their frequent use and potential contact with various contaminants.

256. Lamborghini, founded by Ferruccio Lamborghini in 1963, originally focused on manufacturing agricultural machinery, particularly tractors. It was only later that the company expanded into producing high-performance sports cars, becoming one of the most iconic names in the luxury automobile industry.

257. Jesus in the Bible was not called Jesus by either his disciples or his parents. His actual name was Yeshua or Yehoshua.

The name Jesus is Latin, and it was used when the Roman Empire became Christian. Matthew's original name was "Mattityahu" or "Matityahu".

258. Recycling one ton of paper can save approximately 17-18 trees.

259. Pablo Picasso was a Spanish painter. His full name was Pablo Diego José Francisco de Paula Juan Nepomuceno María de los Remedios Cipriano de la Santísima Trinidad Ruiz y Picasso

260. Jerry Lee Lewis has a pioneering figure in rock music, known for his dynamic performances and songs like "Great Balls of Fire." His career faced a significant setback when he married his 13-year-old cousin, Myra Gale Brown, when he was 22 years old. Importantly, he was still legally married to his first wife, Dorothy Barton, whom he had married when he was 17. This marriage scandal had a lasting impact on his career and reputation.

261. The religious origin of the Christmas tree has ancient roots in human history. The worship of trees was common among pagan Europeans, and this tradition persisted after their conversion to Christianity.

For instance, during the days of celebrating the winter solstice, it was customary to set up a Christmas tree at an entrance or inside a house. Evergreen trees, such as firs, were used as sacred symbols.

When the British royal family used a decorated fir tree for Christmas in 1841, it paved the way for the modern popularity of the evergreen Christmas tree.

Germany's Nazis had no issue with Christmas trees since they have roots in pagan, Germanic traditions. However, Hitler didn't approve of the star at the top of the tree. Instead, Germans could place a swastika or other symbols.

262. Albert Einstein died in the USA in 1955. Dr. Thomas Stoltz Harvey, the pathologist who performed Einstein's autopsy, did indeed remove Einstein's brain during the autopsy for examination, which was a standard procedure. However, instead of returning the brain to the skull, he preserved it in formaldehyde and took it with him. This decision was somewhat unusual and later led to a mix of controversies and scientific studies regarding the examination of Einstein's brain and its potential insights into his genius.

263. On April 1st, 2003, Sitra Walker called her employer and claimed that a robbery was taking place at the store where she worked. The boss called the police. Shortly after, Sitra called back and yelled "APRIL FOOL'S!" The police did not appreciate this and pressed charges against her.

Randy Wood called his ex-wife and convinced her to drive over to his house. When she arrived, she saw Randy hanging from a tree with a rope around his neck.

She was in shock and called the emergency hotline, which dispatched an ambulance. Randy wasn't dead - it was an April Fools' prank.

264. Dennis Hawkins robbed a bank, disguising himself as a woman in the hope of avoiding recognition. He wore a wig and plastic breasts for the disguise but forgot to remove his beard.

265. Tiberius, the Roman Emperor, is known to have indulged in lavish and often debaucherous activities during his reign. His preference for assessing his advisors based on their drinking capacity and participation in sexual activities, as well as his activities on the island of Capri, are documented in historical accounts. Similarly, Emperor Caligula, who succeeded Tiberius, was known for his excessive behavior, including sexual exploits and unusual relationships

266. In France, for a long time, a guillotine was used to execute people. The last person executed using this method was on September 10, 1977.

This refers to executions carried out by authorities as a punishment - not the last person to die by a guillotine, as that happened in 2003. A 36-year-old named Taylor had spent a long time constructing a guillotine. He used it to commit suicide.

267. To sail the Titanic, the ship required 600 tons of coal per day. 100 tons of ash were disposed of into the sea every day.

The ship had 20 lifeboats with a total capacity of 1,178 passengers. There were 2,208 people on board. In total, 1,503 died, and 705 people survived. Two dogs also survived.

There were life jackets available for everyone, but many died due to the cold water.

The last survivor was Millvina Dean. She passed away on May 31, 2009. Millvina was nine weeks old when the Titanic sank in 1912.

The company that built the Titanic also constructed a nearly identical ship called the Olympic. However, Olympic had enough lifeboats for everyone. Olympic collided with a smaller ship on May 15, 1934.

268. Ezra Warner invented the can opener in 1858, which was around 48 years after the invention of canned food. The can opener played a crucial role in making canned goods more accessible and practical for consumers. Prior to the invention of the can opener, opening canned food

required tools like chisels and hammers, making it a cumbersome process.

269. Twerking is a dance style characterized by rhythmic movements of the hips and buttocks. While twerking has gained popularity in modern American culture, its origins are influenced by various dance styles and music genres and have connections to African and Caribbean dance traditions

270. The Spanish flu was an influenza pandemic that started in 1918 and didn't end until 1920. The disease claimed the lives of up to 50 million people, surpassing the death toll of World War I.

Although named the Spanish flu, it didn't necessarily originate in Spain, and its spread was not limited to Spain alone. The influenza strain, also known as H1N1, got its name because Spain was one of the first countries to widely report on it.

American scientists have recreated the virus for the purpose of studying it and have found that it shares similarities with existing contemporary influenza viruses.

271. In December 1948, Costa Rican President José Figueres Ferrer abolished the country's military forces after a civil war known as the Costa Rican Civil War. The decision to redirect military funds to education and culture was a significant step in Costa Rica's history and has contributed to

the country's reputation as a peaceful and stable nation in a region where military conflicts have been more common.

272. In Saudi Arabia, there are no minimum requirements for the age of a bride. A divorce between an 8-year-old girl and her 58-year-old husband was denied by the court

273. The United States' moon landing in 1969 is widely accepted as an authentic event by an overwhelming majority of the U.S. population, with approximately 95% or more of Americans believing in its authenticity.

274. Frederick W. Smith used four million dollars of his own money, raised an additional 90 million, and in 1971 founded the transportation company FedEx.

Three years later, the funds were almost depleted, and absolutely no one wanted to invest more money in the company. There were only 5,000 dollars left in the treasury.

Smith took those 5,000 dollars and flew to Las Vegas. Over the weekend, he won enough in blackjack to keep FedEx afloat for a few more days.

This was enough for FedEx to secure 11 million dollars in funding. FedEx is now one of the world's largest companies in the package delivery industry.

275. The belief that children become hyperactive after consuming sugar is a myth. In experiments, some children were given sugar while others were not. Mothers were told that all the children had received sugar. Most mothers reported that their children were hyperactive whether they had consumed sugar or not.

In another experiment, children were given sugar but mothers were told it was something else. The mothers reported that the children's behavior did not change.

However, if they are given sugar in the form of cola, they become active. This is due to the caffeine, not the sugar.

276. Many people believe that penguins only live in Antarctica and can only survive in cold environments. This is not accurate. Penguins can be found in Chile, Peru, Argentina, Namibia, South Africa, the Galapagos Islands, Australia, and New Zealand.

277. The name "Netherlands" comes from the country's geographical features. The term "Netherlands" translates to "low lands" or "low countries" in English. This name reflects the fact that a significant portion of the country's land is situated at or below sea level. The Netherlands is known for its intricate system of dikes, polders, and water management techniques that have been developed over centuries to reclaim and protect land from the sea. The name accurately describes the country's

flat and often marshy terrain.

278. Earth's rotation is slowing down, but the change is extremely gradual and not easily noticeable on human timescales. The slowing of Earth's rotation is primarily caused by tidal interactions with the Moon. As the Earth's rotation slows down, the length of a day increases, although the change is very minor over the course of a year. This phenomenon is known as "tidal braking."

279. During the medieval period in Europe, the belief in a flat Earth was not as prevalent as often thought. This misconception had largely been dispelled by the 5th century BCE among the ancient Greeks. Notably, Eratosthenes, a Greek mathematician and astronomer, accurately estimated the Earth's circumference to be around 39,250 kilometers, a remarkably close approximation to the modern measurement of approximately 40,075 kilometers at the equator. The prevailing understanding in Europe during this era was that the Earth was a spherical object.

This view was not only embraced by the Church's theologians but also echoed in other cultural and religious contexts. For instance, in the Jewish scriptures, the book of Isaiah 40:22, which dates back to the 8th century BCE, refers to the Earth as a circle. This collective acknowledgment underscores that the recognition of the Earth's spherical shape was a shared understanding across diverse cultures, rather than being confined to a particular geographical or ideological sphere.

280. Christopher Columbus aimed to sail around the Earth to reach India by sailing westward, capitalizing on the understanding that the Earth is spherical.

However, he miscalculated the Earth's circumference, believing it to be much smaller. This led him to think that reaching India by sailing west would be a relatively straightforward journey.

During the voyage, Columbus took measurements of their progress, and it became evident that something was amiss. He had to inform his crew that they were sailing at a slower pace than he initially assumed, and thus they hadn't traveled as far as expected to reach India.

Ultimately, on October 12, 1492, Columbus discovered the Americas. It's worth noting that Vikings had previously discovered America around the year 1018.

281. Lead is a heavy metal that is surprisingly easy to work with. The Romans were among the first to use lead, employing it to create pipes for water transportation. However, a portion of the lead would leach into the water.

As it's well known, the Romans had a fondness for wine and would often consume up to 2 liters a day. However, the wine they drank was diluted and did not have the same alcohol content as modern wines. Nonetheless, this led to another issue.

Lead was introduced into the production of wine. Grape juice, for example, was boiled in lead vessels to concentrate the juice. The lead imparted a sweeter taste to the wine, which was popular among the wealthy and emperors. Lead was also used in cooking other foods for its sweetening and preserving properties.

The effects of lead poisoning include symptoms such as stomach pain, fatigue, depression, constipation, kidney issues, memory loss, aggressive behavior, and sleep problems.

For children, the effects are even more severe, including lower IQ, learning difficulties, hyperactivity, impaired concentration, anxiety, antisocial behavior, and later fertility problems.

Bones from Roman graveyards indicate lead content three times higher than what WHO recommends today.

This history sheds light on the Romans' behaviors and practices, which may appear odd or amusing to us now, but it's crucial to recognize the serious health consequences associated with their exposure to lead.

282. Throughout history, lead has been used in various applications, including paint. In 1921, Thomas Midgley Jr. from General Motors discovered that adding lead to gasoline significantly improved engine performance. He adamantly claimed that lead in gasoline posed no health risks.

However, the truth is that both Midgley himself and his colleagues who worked with lead at General Motors experienced significant health issues due to lead poisoning.

The use of lead in gasoline continued, leading to a steady increase in airborne lead concentration, especially in urban areas.

It wasn't until 1970 that it was recognized that even small amounts of lead caused irreversible damage, particularly to children and fetuses. Data showed that children grew up with altered behavior, learning abilities, and the effects mentioned in the previous point. Lead poisoning inflicts irreversible harm, and no, there's no "detox" regimen with herbs or other remedies that can reverse it. Some countries still allow the use of leaded gasoline.

If your children think you're acting foolishly, it might be worth considering whether their concerns have merit.

283. The name "Pokemon" comes from "pocket monsters."

284. In the past, the city of New York had a different name: New Amsterdam. This change occurred because the city was initially established by the Dutch in 1624. However, the English gained control of the city in 1664 and decided to rename it New York, as a tribute to the English city of York.

Speaking of York, its history stretches back quite far. Originally named "Eoforwic" in Old English, the city's story includes a period when Vikings took over and called it "Jorvik." Over time, this name transformed into the York we know today.

285. At the beginning of the 20th century, Americans were the third tallest in the world. Now they are the 37th tallest. Their diet is attributed to this decline in average height. Fast food, in particular, is blamed for this. On the other hand, they have indeed become wider.

286. In April 2016, at Tokyo Medical University Hospital, doctors were performing a surgery on a woman. The operation was focused on her pelvic area, and a laser was being used, which is a common practice to control bleeding.

Suddenly, the woman apparently released a large fart, which caused the laser to ignite a small fire around the patient.

An expert panel investigated the case and ruled out any other causes except for the presence of intestinal gases.

287. A company in the USA issues insurance policies against alien abductions. The policy costs $19.95 and pays out $10 million if you are abducted. You must be able to provide evidence of the abduction.

288. Colombia is the world's largest producer of narcotics, excluding nicotine in tobacco as a narcotic.

More Colombians die from American tobacco than there are Americans dying from Colombian narcotics.

289. In ancient Greece, the term "idiotes" was used to describe individuals who were not involved in public affairs or political life. It was used to denote someone who focused solely on their private interests and did not participate in civic duties or responsibilities. The term's meaning has evolved over time to refer to someone who is foolish or lacks intelligence, but its original usage was more closely tied to political engagement.

290. In 1492, the Pope was named Innocent VIII. The name can be translated to "innocent," but he was not.

He was very ill in 1492, and no doctor could help him. An Italian historian recounts that, in an effort to aid the Pope, some boys were drained of blood. That is, all of their blood was drained until they died. This was believed to transfer their youthful vitality into the blood.

The Pope was to drink the blood while it was still fresh and warm, in the hope of absorbing the young boys' life force.

291. If you found the above information a bit gross, you might find the following even more nauseating.

During the Middle Ages, doctors recommended the consumption of medicines made from mummies. Ideally, these would be high-quality mummies from Egypt, but there was a lot of deception, and ordinary corpses were often used. Drying them in the sun or an oven could make them look indistinguishable. The mummies were crushed and ingested.

Starting from the 16th century, however, doctors began to argue that fresh corpses were far superior, as they contained a life force that didn't immediately vanish upon death. Everything was used—menstrual blood, blood, brains, placenta, and crushed bones. Breast milk from a young girl to adult individuals was also considered effective against signs of aging.

When a criminal was executed, their body could be sold to doctors. Spectators often eagerly collected the blood flowing from the executed person and immediately drank it, believing it to be rich in life force.

What people didn't know was that blood could also contain a multitude of viruses.

The concept of this kind of cannibalism faded away during the 18th century—or did it?

292. In the 1970s, it became popular to consume the placenta after childbirth, specifically a woman's own placenta. In recent years, this

practice has gained popularity among celebrities. For instance, two Kardashian sisters have reportedly consumed their own placentas.

The idea behind this trend was that by ingesting the placenta, one could potentially prevent postpartum depression and aid the woman's body in recovering after childbirth.

Various recipes involving placenta were created (remember the salt). Some people preferred placenta smoothies, which could be blended with fruits. Placenta could also be dried and turned into pills.

However, there is no scientific evidence to support the notion that consuming placenta is beneficial for health.

293. HIV (Human Immunodeficiency Virus) has two main types, HIV-1 and HIV-2, and it is believed to have originated from primates in Africa, particularly chimpanzees. The transmission from primates to humans likely occurred through hunting and consumption of primate meat. HIV has indeed evolved in the human population, leading to the global pandemic. The estimated number of people living with HIV globally was around 37.6 million, according to the Joint United Nations Programme on HIV/AIDS (UNAIDS).

294 The "Three Hundred and Thirty-Five Years' War" is a term used to describe a theoretical state of war between the Isles of Scilly (part of the UK) and the Netherlands.

The war began in 1651 during the English Civil War, and its theoretical duration spanned 335 years. The "war" only formally ended in 1986 when a peace treaty was humorously signed. No casualties occurred during the duration of this so-called war, and no shots were ever fired.

The situation gained widespread attention in 1985, when Roy Duncan, Chairman of the Isles of Scilly Council, was informed about the "state of war" by a local historian. As a result of this awareness, the Dutch ambassador, Rein Huydecoper, visited the Isles of Scilly in 1986, and a peace treaty was playfully signed, marking the "end" of the "war."

295. Bluetooth is a way for computers to communicate with other computers and electronic systems.

It is named after the Danish Viking Harald Bluetooth. The symbol/logo for Bluetooth is composed of the runic characters for "H" and "B."

296. Elvis Presley (January 8, 1935 – August 16, 1977) appeared in 33 films and sold over a billion records worldwide. He recorded hundreds of songs but did not write any of them himself.

297. Spiridon Louis won the first modern Olympic marathon in the 1896 Athens Olympics. He wasn't a professional runner but was a water carrier by profession. He was reported to have stopped during the race to have an orange and possibly some brandy, which was a common practice among athletes in those times. He completed the marathon in a time of

about 2 hours, 58 minutes, and 50 seconds.

298. There's no longer an excuse not to climb Mount Everest, at least not the excuse of needing to check emails.

In 2010, a Nepalese telecommunications company installed cell towers, allowing people to access the internet. After all, people need to be able to send a selfie from the top of the mountain.

Thousands of people have climbed the mountain, resulting in the need to remove several tons of waste. Waste remains a significant problem on the mountain.

The mountain stands at 8,850 meters (29,035 feet) tall and grows by about four millimeters per year.

299. The term "kosher" designates foods that are permitted for Jews to eat according to the laws outlined in the Mosaic books and Jewish tradition. For instance, they are not allowed to consume pork, horse, shellfish, mollusks, and other items.

To assist consumers in identifying what Jews are allowed to eat, foods undergo certification.

Stamps are certified as "kosher" in Israel.

300. Japan has faced significant challenges related to suicide rates. The country has one of the highest suicide rates in the world, with various factors contributing to this issue. Social pressures, economic difficulties, cultural stigmas, and mental health struggles have played roles in the prevalence of suicide in Japan. The Japanese government and various organizations have implemented initiatives to address this serious concern and provide support for those in need. Efforts are being made to raise awareness about mental health, reduce the stigma surrounding seeking help, and improve access to mental health services to curb the high suicide rates in the country.

301. The invention of the lottery cannot be attributed to a single individual, as various forms of lotteries have been practiced throughout history by different cultures and societies. Lotteries have ancient origins and have been used for various purposes, including raising funds for public projects, social events, and even religious rituals. One of the earliest recorded lotteries dates back to ancient China during the Han Dynasty around 205 BC. Lotteries have evolved over time and have been used by different civilizations for different purposes.

302. Jack Whittaker won the equivalent of around 750 million Danish kroner in a lottery in 2002. However, Jack's luck took a turn for the worse. He was unlucky to experience three robberies within a short period of time.

His granddaughter's boyfriend died of a drug overdose, and the granddaughter herself died after a kidnapping. Unfortunately, he also lost a lot of money through gambling, his daughter died suddenly, and his house burned down. It's worth noting that the house was not insured.

303. One of the luckiest men in the world is Frank Selak from Croatia. He experienced seven disasters in which he narrowly escaped death.

The first incident occurred in 1962 when he was traveling by train from Sarajevo to Dubrovnik. The train derailed and plunged into an icy river. Seventeen people drowned, but he survived with shock and a broken arm.

The following year, he was thrown out of an airplane when the door fell off. Nineteen people died, but he survived by landing in a haystack.

In 1966, the bus he was traveling on overturned into another river.

In 1970, his car caught fire on a highway, and three years later, his car caught fire again.

In 1995, he was hit by a bus, and the following year he experienced another car accident when his Skoda went off a cliff.

At the age of 74, he won in a lottery. It was the first lottery he had ever participated in.

304. In the entire state of Ohio, USA, in the year 1895, there were only two cars. It is said that oth of them were involved in a car accident as they collided with each other.

305. The world's largest kidney stone weighed nearly 1.5 kilograms. (3,3 pounds)

306. Ducks are among the most sexually aggressive birds. It's not uncommon for one or more male ducks (drakes) to suddenly gang up and sexually assault a female duck.

As this often takes place in water, the victim can end up drowning since the male duck frequently holds her head underwater.

307 When researchers are bored, they conduct strange studies. One such study revealed that if men wear a white T-shirt with the letter "T" written on the front, they become 10% more attractive to women.

Researchers at Nottingham Trent University believe this phenomenon is due to the increased chest-to-waist ratio, making the men appear more masculine. They even experimented with T-shirts featuring a reversed "T," and allegedly, women found men wearing these T-shirts less attractive.

308. Thai woman Ann Kamsuk died in a traffic accident. At the time, she was in a relationship with TV producer Chadil Deffy, who decided to marry Ann on the same day as her funeral.

Wearing mourning attire, Chadil said his vows and placed the ring on Ann's stiff, lifeless finger. He documented the ceremony/funeral with photos and videos, which were shared over 50,000 times on the internet via Facebook and YouTube.

Chadil and Ann had been in a relationship for 10 years, and she passed away before he decided to marry her. Was it a sweet gesture or a media stunt?

Mr. Lai in Taiwan did a similar thing, though without the involvement of Facebook and YouTube. He married a woman after she had passed away and been cremated. The urn even had a bridal gown on.

309. Timothy Leary was an American psychologist who recommended psychedelic substances for various purposes, such as administering certain drugs to prisoners to alter their behavior. He participated in experiments with inmates involving such substances.

In 1968, he was arrested for possession of marijuana. While in jail, he underwent a test to determine the type of work he could perform while incarcerated. Those conducting the test were unaware that Leary himself had designed it, so he answered in a way that led to him being assigned outdoor gardening work and low-security checks. He managed to escape.

310. Lawrence Richard Walters later got the nickname "Lawnchair Larry". He was a truck driver which apparently wasn't thrilling enough, and Lawrence had always dreamed of flying. Now was the time.

In 1982, he acquired 45 weather balloons. He filled them with helium and tied them to a regular lawn chair.

Lawrence flew approximately 4,500 meters up in the air. He floated around up there for a while, disturbing air traffic in the process.

He flew around for 45 minutes before descending and getting stuck in some power lines, from which he had to be helped down.

The incident cost him a fine of $1,500.

311. Mike Tyson, the former professional boxer, is known for many things, and among them is a distinctive tribal tattoo on his face. The tattoo, which covers the left side of his face, was inked in 2003 and quickly became one of his most recognized features. Tyson's tattoo artist, Victor Whitmill, later sued Warner Bros. for replicating the design on actor Ed Helms's face in the movie "The Hangover Part II" without permission.

312. Several airlines now require overweight people to purchase an extra plane seat.

313. "Juice is healthy, right? That's what people say, but you probably shouldn't drink too much of it. There are more calories in juices and smoothies than in sodas.

A soda usually has 42 kcal per 100 ml, but apple juice has 47 kcal per ml. Both drinks contain carbohydrates.

I've always said beer is better. Depending on the type of beer, there are only about 38 kcal per 100 ml, and beer is rich in B-vitamins, magnesium, and silica.

So be careful not to get a big "juice belly."

314. In 1964, the city council of Kuwait City faced a significant issue. A heavy cargo ship had sunk in the harbor. Authorities needed to devise a method to raise and remove this ship.

Kuwait City's city council sought outside help, and Danish inventor Karl Krøyer contacted Kuwait's authorities with a brilliant idea.

He proposed using a massive quantity of plastic spheres. These spheres would be pumped into the ship, causing it to rise to the surface. He named these spheres "Krøyer balls." Surprisingly, the method worked, and the ship resurfaced.

News of Krøyer's remarkable invention spread worldwide, and along the coast of Greenland, there was also a ship in need of salvaging. Once again, the Krøyer balls proved to be successful.

Krøyer applied for a patent for his method and received approvals in the United Kingdom and Germany. However, things went awry in the Netherlands. The Dutch patent court rejected his application, stating that they had seen Krøyer's salvaging method before—in a Donald Duck comic.

In 1949, Donald Duck had used a very similar method to raise a ship. They used ping pong balls instead, which meant that the difference wasn't substantial enough for Krøyer to obtain a patent for the salvaging method.

315. In 1875, the king of Fiji went on a state visit to Australia. During his visit, he contracted measles, which he brought back home. This resulted in a quarter of his population dying.

316. King Richard I, commonly known as Richard the Lionheart, ruled from 1189 to 1199. He is renowned for his chivalry, military prowess, and his involvement in the Third Crusade. One of the most intriguing aspects of his life is his capture, ransom, and the tales of his adventures during his imprisonment.

During his return journey from the Holy Land after the Crusades, Richard was captured in 1192 by Leopold V, Duke of Austria. He was subsequently handed over to Holy Roman Emperor Henry VI and held captive in a castle in the Austrian Alps.

Richard's captivity became the subject of legends and stories. One of the most famous stories involves a minstrel named Blondel. According to the legend, Blondel traveled from castle to castle, singing a specific song that only he and Richard knew. The story goes that when Blondel finally reached the castle where Richard was held, the King heard the song and responded with the correct lines, revealing his presence. This loyal minstrel played a role in helping to locate the captive King.

Richard's release came at a high cost. His younger brother, John, who was acting as regent in England, negotiated a massive ransom to secure Richard's freedom. The equivalent of an enormous sum in today's currency was paid to the Holy Roman Emperor. Richard was released in 1194.

317. Andrew Carnegie, a Scottish-American industrialist and philanthropist, is well-known for his immense wealth amassed from the steel industry. What many might not know is that he used a significant portion of his fortune to establish public libraries.

Carnegie's passion for education and access to knowledge led him to fund the construction of over 2,500 public libraries worldwide, with the majority located in the United States. His philanthropic efforts greatly contributed to the expansion of public education and literacy, allowing countless individuals to access books and resources that they might not have otherwise had the opportunity to explore.

318. Saudi Arabia has one of the world's largest deserts. What you probably didn't expect is that Saudi Arabia actually imports sand. The reason is that the type of sand they have is not suitable for the construction industry

319. It is commonly known that ancient Ninja warriors wore black outfits, but they never did. This is a myth from the world of movies.

This would not be a very effective method for moving unnoticed among people. Instead, they would dress completely like the local population

320. Tobacco is harmful to people, both through direct smoking and indirect passive smoking. However, it was also because of tobacco that the slave trade in America began.

Tobacco was popular in Europe, especially in England. It led the first American inhabitants to start growing tobacco. The climate was suitable, and they lacked a good export commodity to trade for things they couldn't yet produce in America. The English were fond of smoking, which was in high fashion. The problem was that their rival, Spain, grew a lot of tobacco, and they didn't want to financially support Spain.

The first approximately 20 African slaves arrived in Jamestown in 1612. They were to be used for cultivating tobacco for the settlers, who could sell it to England. In the 1700s, the slave trade exploded, and Africans were used to cultivate tobacco, cotton, and sugar.

Denmark began trading in slaves when the Danish West India Guinea Company was established in 1674. The company transported and sold around 100,000 slaves.

Denmark was the first country in the world to ban the slave trade in 1792. It was Christian VII who issued the "Ordinance on the Negro Trade." So, the regulation was about the trade itself. Slavery itself was banned in Denmark in 1848.

However, the trade in African slaves was not the first time Denmark was involved in slavery. Already during the Viking Age, slavery was practiced in Denmark, although not with Africans.

321. Creating a bestseller book like this usually involves hard work. However, not in 1956 when the book "I, Libertine" by Frederick Ewing hit the New York Times bestseller list even before its release.

However, the situation was that the book didn't actually exist. It was the author Jean Shepherd who had started the hoax, meant as a little joke. On his radio show, he had talked about some of the plot of this book and encouraged people to request it from bookstores.

He expected it to confuse a couple of booksellers, but the book - the non-existent book - took on a life of its own. It was mentioned on other radio shows and in book clubs, and people began to reserve the book at bookstores, so the book ended up on the New York Times bestseller list.

322. The body contains billions of bacteria, and we usually don't notice them. In 2013, a man went to the hospital and was incredibly drunk. The strange thing was that he hadn't consumed any alcohol. He was kept in a hospital room for 24 hours and was given food and water. Normally, a person automatically becomes sober, but this man's blood alcohol level increased!

After further investigation, it turned out that his gut flora contained Saccharomyces cerevisiae, which is yeast that converts sugar and starch into alcohol. Normally, this yeast dies in the stomach, but in some individuals, it happily lives in the intestines, effectively turning the person into a human brewery. It doesn't get cheaper than that.

323. The invention of the modern hamburger is often attributed to the United States, specifically to the early 20th century. Although various cultures had meat-based dishes that can be considered precursors to the hamburger, it was in the U.S. that the concept of placing a ground beef patty between two pieces of bread became popularized. The origin of the term "hamburger" is linked to Hamburg, Germany, where a type of seasoned minced beef called "Hamburg steak" was well-known. However, it was American innovations like the fast-food industry and the establishment of White Castle, often credited as the first fast-food hamburger chain, that contributed to the widespread popularity of hamburgers as we know them today.

324. In the state of Oregon, Saccharomyces cerevisiae is apparently important. They have designated this microbe as the official "state

microbe." They believe this yeast is important for people's quality of life.

325. From 1920 to 1933, alcohol was prohibited to drink throughout the entire United States. It was said to reduce crime. However, it directly contributed to the rise of the mafia in the U.S., but that's a different story.

Prohibition led to the creation of another product, namely pure grape concentrate. People could drink it like fruit juice. Of course, there was the risk that the juice would ferment and turn into wine if not handled carefully.

To warn people about this "risk," they added a clear warning label on the packaging. The warning contained detailed instructions about what NOT to do. Otherwise, there was a risk of inadvertently turning it into alcohol.

326. Peter the Great, who ruled the Tsardom of Russia from 1682 to 1725, is known for his efforts to modernize and Westernize Russia.

Peter the Great had a strong preference for Western customs and fashion. As part of his efforts to modernize Russia's appearance and culture, he encouraged men to adopt a clean-shaven look, which was more common in Western Europe at the time.

To discourage the wearing of beards, Peter the Great imposed a beard tax. Those who wanted to keep their beards had to pay the tax, which was enforced as a way to promote a clean-shaven appearance.

This policy was symbolic of Peter the Great's broader efforts to reform and modernize various aspects of Russian society and culture.

327. "Space Invaders" is a classic arcade video game released in 1978 by Taito, a Japanese video game company. It was one of the earliest shooting games and became a major success.

The popularity of "Space Invaders" in Japan was indeed significant during the late 1970s and early 1980s. It became a cultural phenomenon and had a substantial impact on the video game industry.

Due to the popularity of the game, there were reports of shortages of 100-yen coins in Japan, as players flocked to arcades to play "Space Invaders." This led to authorities issuing additional coins to meet the demand.

The success of "Space Invaders" contributed to the rise of video games as a form of entertainment and paved the way for the growth of the arcade industry.

328. Vladimir Lenin was hailed by many as the one who singlehandedly liberated Russia from czarist rule. However, without financial support from the German Emperor Wilhelm II, the 1917 revolution might not have materialized.

The German government disbursed substantial sums in 1915, through an intermediary in Copenhagen, to the Russian Bolsheviks. The money was used for weapons for the Russian Bolsheviks, who were causing disturbances.

The plan succeeded. Two years after the initial German millions were paid to the Bolsheviks, the czar was killed.

329. There was technological development during World War II, but not everything worked equally well.

The Germans had built a significant number of submarines, posing a great threat to the Allies. However, the German submarine U-1206 didn't require much effort to combat. The crew managed to do that on the submarine's first voyage.

The reason for the submarine's sinking was that the crew had used the toilet incorrectly. The toilet was designed for use while the submarine was submerged deep in the sea. But when the submarine was at significant depths, the toilet had to be operated in a specific manner due to the high pressure at those depths.

The contents of the toilet were supposed to be ejected from the submarine, almost like a kind of fecal torpedo. This is where things went wrong. The captain needed to use the toilet, but it wasn't flushed in the correct way.

Water began to flood into the submarine through the toilet. The water hit some batteries, causing them to emit toxic chlorine gas. The submarine had to surface.

The submarine was discovered and sunk by the British. Four men died, and the rest were captured.

330. At one point, South Africa was occupied by the British. A teenage girl from the Xhosa people had a dream that explained how they could overcome the occupation.

She dreamt that they should kill all the cattle and burn the crops. This prophetic dream reached the ears of the chief, who ordered the cattle to be killed and the crops to be burned. This resulted in a massive famine among the Xhosa people, leading to the death of around 40,000 individuals. This can indeed be considered a nightmare.

331. The cheapest method for determining your race might be the South African pencil test.

During apartheid (racial segregation) in South Africa, determining someone's race was often based on their skin color. However, there were individuals with parents of different races, and they could have relatively lighter skin. What about them? They might have had grandparents of a different race. How could people be categorized?

The pencil test was simple, cost-effective, and considered efficient. It involved inserting a pencil into a person's hair. The race category was determined based on how easily the pencil could be dislodged. You see, Africans have thick, coarse hair that can hold onto various objects.

If the pencil fell out easily, you were considered white. If it stayed put, you were categorized as black. If it could fall out when shaking your head, you were considered colored or of mixed race.

In 2016, there were demonstrations in South Africa over certain schools requiring black individuals to have specific approved hairstyles and not allowing "afro hair."

332. Boxing gloves were introduced as a safety measure to protect the hands of boxers and reduce facial injuries that were common when bare-knuckle fighting was prevalent.

The use of gloves in boxing aimed to make the sport safer by minimizing facial cuts and injuries, which were common in bare-knuckle fighting due to the sharper impact on the skin.

Brain injuries in boxing, such as concussions and chronic traumatic encephalopathy (CTE), are caused by repeated and forceful blows to the head, regardless of whether gloves are worn or not. The cumulative effect of these impacts over time is what contributes to long-term brain damage.

Brain injuries in boxing were prevalent even during the bare-knuckle era, albeit they might not have been as well-documented.

333. The main task of the United Nations Security Council is to ensure peace and security in the world. The Security Council can initiate negotiations among conflicting parties, call for and negotiate ceasefires, impose economic sanctions, and deploy UN forces. It has five permanent members: the United Kingdom, the United States, France, China, and Russia.

As a side note, I can inform you that the largest exporters of military weapons in the world are the United Kingdom, the United States, France, China, Germany, and Russia.

334. Newborn babies cannot see colors at all. They can only see colors after a few months, so they are completely indifferent to whether girls wear pink and boys wear blue.

In fact, it wasn't always this way. It was the opposite. The slightly wild color of pink was associated with boys and men, while the color blue was considered mild and calm, making it suitable for girls. A French writer recommended in 1794 that men paint their rooms pink and white to uplift their spirits.

It wasn't until the 1940s that the color choice began to shift. This change is believed to be due to the fashion industry, which decided that blue should be associated with boys.

335. What's worse than boys wearing pink was that both boys and girls wore dresses. There are thousands of photos of boys in dresses and even with long hair.

In many historical cultures, including Western cultures, it was common for both young boys and girls to wear dresses or similar clothing styles until they reached a certain age, usually around the age of 6 or 7.

Dresses were considered practical for young children because they allowed for easier movement and were more adaptable to growth.

The practice of dressing young boys and girls in similar styles began to change in the late 19th and early 20th centuries, as cultural norms and fashion trends evolved.

336. For decades, there has been a fight against drugs. In the 1990s, an idea emerged in the USA to write "Too cool to do drugs" on school pencils. The intention was good, but then children and teenagers started using the pencils.

Pencils need to be sharpened from time to time. The sentence was thus gradually shortened, over time becoming "cool to do drugs," and later simply ending up as "do drugs."

337. Once again in the USA: In 2010, the United States Postal Service issued a postage stamp. The intention was to feature an image of the Statue of Liberty from New York.

However, the designers made a mistake. They accidentally purchased an image of the Statue of Liberty from "Getty Images," an online photo service. The image was of a Statue of Liberty, but not the original one. It turned out to be a picture of a replica of the Statue of Liberty located in Las Vegas.

Several billion of these postage stamps have been sold, and they are still in circulation.

338. The definition of "perseverance" is now clarified by a 69-year-old Korean woman. She failed her driving test hundreds of times before finally passing.

Cha Sa-Soon took the test multiple times a week but couldn't succeed. She simply couldn't pass the written exam. When she finally passed that, she also had to pass the practical driving test. It took her 8 attempts before she succeeded.

During all the time it took her, Cha became nationally known for her perseverance, and Hyundai gifted her a car. I wouldn't dare to guess the insurance premium.

339. We witness European determination in the Czech Republic. In 2012, a Czech gang stole a 10-ton metal bridge along with some railway tracks. Everything was sold as scrap metal.

The gang had forged documents from the authorities stating that the bridge needed replacement and that there would be construction work in the area.

Similar incidents have occurred in Turkey. In this case, a 22-ton bridge was stolen.

340. The Great Pacific Garbage Patch is a collection of marine debris, primarily consisting of plastic, in the central North Pacific Ocean. It is often referred to as the "largest landfill in the world" due to its vast size and the accumulation of waste.

Plastic waste is a major component of the debris in the Great Pacific Garbage Patch, with estimates suggesting that plastic constitutes a substantial portion, possibly around 90% of the waste.

341. The world's oldest kingdom, as we all know, is Denmark. The world's youngest kingdom is the Kingdom of North Sudan, established in 2014.

Jeremiah Heaton traveled to a small area called Bir Tawil, located between Egypt and Sudan. It's a mountainous no-man's land without fertile soil, neither Egypt nor Sudan wanting to claim it due to disputes over another nearby area and issues related to historical border treaties. In other words, there were a lot of political complications.

While in the area, Jeremiah planted a flag and declared the land to be his kingdom, making his 7-year-old daughter a princess. However, this kingdom is not internationally recognized.

342. If you have an old-fashioned shortwave radio, you might be fortunate enough to listen to some mysterious broadcasts between 3 and 30 MHz. Across the world, broadcasts can be intercepted featuring a mechanical voice reciting sequences of numbers. Nobody knows where these transmissions originate from or their purpose, as their source cannot be traced. The exact start date is also unknown, but these broadcasts are said to have existed for at least a human generation.

There are theories that these broadcasts could potentially be related to espionage data from World War I or II, but no governments have admitted to their origin. Furthermore, the question remains as to why these broadcasts haven't been shut down. The purpose behind these transmissions and why they persist remains unexplained by any theory.

Despite their powerful signals, they remain untraceable. How can they persist for so many decades? Electronic devices emitting radio waves would presumably wear out, and how do they continue to receive power? How has the secrecy been maintained for such a long period?

Efforts are ongoing to uncover the meaning of these broadcasts, but no one has managed to decipher and decode the significance of the numerical sequences, which to this day continue to be transmitted from undisclosed locations.

343. In 1974, things were about to take an unexpected turn for the residents near Kruzof Island in Alaska, where the dormant volcano Mount Edgecumbe is located. Situated near the volcano, which hadn't erupted in millennia, is a town called Sitka.

But then it happened...

In April 1974, black smoke began to billow from the volcano, visible from a distance. In response, a helicopter was immediately dispatched to investigate and capture images of the volcano's activity. To the pilot's surprise, and perhaps relief, something was visible at the top of the volcano: the words "April Fools."

Oliver Bickar had conceived this idea three years prior and had been preparing for the moment. He had gathered a pile of old tires and waited until the day arrived to set them ablaze.

344 "Wokeness" is a colloquial term that has gained prominence in recent years. It refers to an awareness and activism regarding social and political issues, particularly those related to discrimination, inequality, and social justice. Someone who is "woke" considers themself to be socially

conscious and aware of systemic injustices, especially those related to race, gender, sexuality, and other marginalized identities.

The term "wokeness" has been associated with efforts to challenge and address issues such as racism, sexism, LGBTQ+ rights, environmental concerns, and more. It has been used to describe a heightened sense of awareness and a commitment to advocating for positive change in society.

That was it...

Shall we not say, that's enough? Even though I have plenty of useless knowledge, it has to come to an end at some point.

I hope you've enjoyed the journey and learned something new about the world around you.

***Did you find this book informative?* Please consider giving a review om Amazon, or please mention this book on your social media.**

Thanks, its greatly appreciated.

Find other books at

www.VirtusPublish.com

Printed in Great Britain
by Amazon

31397374R00079